W9-BFY-891

The Essential
BARTENDER'S
Pocket Guide

The Essential
BARTENDER'S
Pocket Guide

Truly Great
Cocktail
Recipes

ROBERT HESS

Mud Puddle Books
NEW YORK

The Essential Bartender's Pocket Guide:
Truly Great Cocktail Recipes
by Robert Hess

Copyright © 2009 by Mud Puddle Books

Published by
Mud Puddle Books, Inc.
54 W. 21st Street
Suite 601
New York, NY 10010
info@mudpuddlebooks.com

ISBN: 978-1-60311-151-5

Portions of this book appeared, in a slightly different format,
in *The Essential Bartender's Guide: How to Create Truly Great Cocktails*
by Robert Hess (Mud Puddle Books, 2008)

Design by Barbara Scott-Goodman
Cover Design by Alan Carr

For complete photographic credits, please see page 178

Printed in China

Table of Contents

Introduction

Cocktails have been enjoyed for more than 200 years, and throughout those 200 years the word cocktail has consistently conjured up different images for different people. A confusion, yes, but a tasty one.

The history of cocktails begins with just a few drinks created by the bartenders of the day. They had such names as the Whiskey Cocktail, Brandy Cocktail, Gin Cocktail, Fancy Whiskey Cocktail, Fancy Brandy Cocktail and Fancy Gin Cocktail. For a while these were just about the extent of available cocktails. But it didn't take long for this simple list to expand to dozens, then hundreds, then thousands of different drinks created by the imaginations of the countless bartenders around the world.

The goal of this pocket guide is to present bartenders, both home and professional, with the information needed to really understand the cocktail and how to properly prepare the best drinks possible. Given straightforward information on preparation and ingredients as well as a touch of the evolutionary history of the cocktail, you can mix a world-class drink. Understanding will take the confusion out of the word cocktail.

Let the journey begin!

BALE OF HAY SALOON   VIRGINIA CITY, MONT.

Cocktail as Cuisine

The cocktail can and should be seen as a cuisine with all the potential and wonder that this implies. Bartenders are masters of this cuisine and should be expected to take their role as seriously as if they were a chef turning out masterful dishes for their customers. Likewise a consumer should approach a cocktail with as much attention to its quality as possible.

Wine, beer and even coffee can be seen as liquid cuisines which embody the notion of craftsmanship, dedication and quality. Like the cocktail, they haven't, however, always been seen as such.

Today, sommeliers are commonplace at restaurants. They help diners create a memorable pairing between the food from the kitchen and the wine from the restaurant's cellar. Drinkers, who would have once seen an inexpensive white zinfandel as their go-to wine now cherish the robust and complex flavors of a cabernet sauvignon or pinot noir.

Across the nation small microbreweries are producing a variety of craft beers full of flavor and character. While the large commercial breweries and their almost flavorless beers are still top sellers, an educated beer drinker is always on the lookout for new and interesting brews to provide their palate with a little adventure.

Once it was believed that great coffee came out of a can and the percolator was the most popular way to brew a cup. Today, there are a variety of gourmet roasters which have created a dedicated consumer base. People may drive miles out of their way to buy coffee. They will grind whole beans at home and carefully brew their coffee to get just the right flavor for their morning cup.

While cocktails haven't yet achieved this level of large scale craftsmanship, dedication and awareness, there is a definite momentum in that direction. Bartenders are enthusiastically studying, researching and training in order to create exquisite cocktails based on classic methods. Customers are seeking out these bartenders and allowing them to provide drink recommendations instead of simply having the same tried-and-true cocktails over and over again.

The "Cocktailian" Palate

The appreciation for unknown flavors is something that we can be open to throughout our lives. There's always a thrill encountering and discovering something new. When we're young and first begin to drink wine, we are unlikely to start with an appreciation of a robust wine like a cabernet sauvignon or zinfandel. Often our choice is a mild sweet wine and the memories of fruit juices and soda pops it produces.

After hiding away in the sweet soda pop wines for a while, we might strive, for example, to impress a date by taking advantage of a sommelier who, by offering an education on the available wines, helps to push our palates forward. Eventually we end up ordering and appreciating the same complex red wines that once sent us running for cover.

Regrettably, there isn't yet the cocktail equivalent of a sommelier, a role model to help our understanding of the culinary potential cocktails can provide. This is why many drinks are closer in a flavor profile to soda pop wines than vintage cabernets.

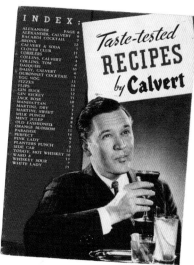

Circa 1950

Balancing Act

Appreciation of the cocktail as a culinary beverage begins with its balance of flavors.

Jigger

Not too sweet, not too sour, not too strong, but something blending all of the presented flavors in a form that creates what could almost be considered a brand new flavor. This "new" flavor should, as you come to the end of your cocktail, bring a wish that the glass contained a little bit more.

For both the bartender and the consumer, the cocktail should represent a great culinary adventure. This recognition and appreciation will return the dignity and stature the cocktail enjoyed nearly a hundred years ago.

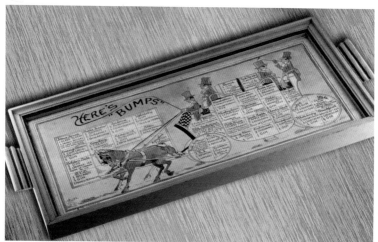
1931

The Tele-Bar was a combination of a 21-inch television, radio, phonograph, and complete bar. 1951.

The Home Bartender

Anybody can select a great wine. Your chances are good even if you randomly pick a bottle for the sole reason that it has a pretty label on it. But a great cocktail can't get into a glass by accident. It takes a certain amount of skill to know how to properly select and combine the right ingredients, and it takes familiarity and awareness to know a truly good thing when you taste it.

Learning how to make great cocktails can be an exceedingly rewarding experience. It can be learned quickly and then savored lovingly as you expend the time necessary to master it.

As you become more and more secure with the cocktails you make at home, you will discover that you'll be able to make far better choices, with knowledge and conviction, when you order cocktails and other mixed drinks at the restaurants and cocktail lounges you might visit.

Making cocktails at home can be a relaxing and decompressing ritual after a long day. It takes a short amount of time to gather your bar equipment, the necessary ingredients and artfully prepare a drink for the evening. The process can provide you with a great opportunity to leave behind all of the pressures of the day. The cocktail itself simply becomes the period at the end of the sentence.

We're now ready to look at the various tools, methods and secrets to making great cocktails at home. We'll see that no shortcuts are necessary and that the home bartender can be as professional as the one at your favorite drinking establishment. We'll discover not only the proper way to make many of the world's most famous cocktails, but why they should be made in a particular way and how it makes a difference.

Viva la Cocktail!

Tools of the Trade

The tools for making a proper cocktail are fairly simple and straightforward. You may even have various things in your kitchen already which can take their place in a pinch. These tools of course are designed to assist you in applying the proper methods and processes when you mix your drinks. Understanding these methods and processes, and having the tools designed for them, will go a long way in making the perfect cocktail.

The Basic Kit

For your bare bones bartending kit, you should pick up the following:

- Jigger
- Cocktail Shaker
- Bar Spoon
- Strainer
- Glassware

Jigger

Cocktail recipes may call for as little as $\frac{1}{4}$ ounce or even a dash for certain ingredients. When measuring small amounts, especially ones with as much flavor as lemon juice, it's crucial to get an accurate measurement. This could be the difference between a great cocktail and a terrible one. Sure, you may see bartenders pouring products

Jiggers

straight from bottles into mixing glasses without seeming to measure them. Trust me, it's not as easy as the bartender makes it appear.

The jiggers generally found in kitchen stores rarely tell you how many ounces they are measuring. This is an obvious problem. Also, their shape is usually conical. This might not pose a problem when you need a full measure, but what if your jigger measures 1 ounce (30ml) and you need ¾ (22ml)? Conical shapes are terrible for eyeballing a partial measure accurately. The best cocktail measures are the ones that clearly and accurately provide measures for up to 2 ounces (60ml) in ¼ ounce (7ml) increments.

Although I usually don't like getting brand specific on products of this nature, I will say that my personal favorite jigger for home use is the OXO Mini Angled Measure. Generally you'll find it with the measuring cups at your local kitchen store rather than the bar tools section.

Cocktail Shaker

There are essentially two types of cocktail shakers. The one most commonly found in kitchen stores is the Combination, sometimes referred to as a Cobbler style shaker. They are also known as Three Part because they consist of three separate parts. The lower part is the mixing tin, the middle part is the cover with an integrated strainer and the third is the cap, which tightly covers the strainer so you can shake up a drink without spilling things. Personally I don't recommend this style of shaker. You'll find that most bars don't use this style either. They don't work effectively, and the middle portion often sticks to the bottom.

The second style is what is commonly known as a Boston Shaker. This consists of a pint glass (a.k.a. mixing glass) and a metal mixing tin. The mixing tin is larger than the pint glass, allowing one to fit tightly within the other. When the shaker is properly sealed, you can quickly and easily shake up any cocktail. You should note that it often takes a little time to gain the experience to properly seal the shaker. Warning: When it isn't properly sealed, you end up with the drink all over yourself, or worse yet, your guests.

A variation of the Boston Shaker is a two part metal shaker with an elegant curve on the top. These are often referred to as Parisian shakers since they were popularized by bartenders in Paris.

My personal recommendation is for the Boston Shaker style. Most of the best bartenders use this and, with just a little practice, it's quite effective.

A few tips for properly using a Boston Shaker: first, measure the liquid ingredients into the pint glass. Put the ice into the metal mixing tin. Then pour the contents of the pint glass into the mixing tin and solidly place the inverted mixing glass over and into the mixing tin. Give the bottom of the glass a solid whack with your palm to seal the two together. Holding the mixing tin tightly in

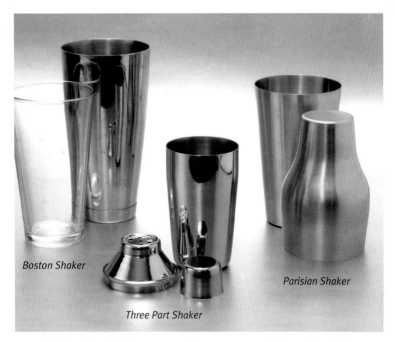

Boston Shaker

Three Part Shaker

Parisian Shaker

your left hand and the mixing glass in your right hand, solidly shake the drink.

When you're finished shaking, hold the mixing tin in your left hand. With the palm of your right hand, give a solid whack to the side of the mixing tin where you imagine the edge of the mixing glass to be. This will almost always separate the two so you can easily strain the drink. It does, however, take a little practice.

Bar Spoon

Since not all drinks need to be shaken, this is a good time to ask "when do I shake?" and "when do I stir?" There's a secret to the answer which few modern bartenders seem to know.

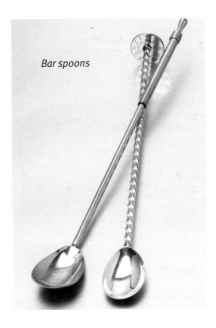

Bar spoons

The purpose of shaking or stirring is to chill the drink as well as provide some dilution of the ice into the drink (which is important!). Both shaking and stirring do an equal job at this. Stirring takes a little longer, however, but shaking dilutes the drink more. In the end, it's all pretty much a wash. The reason you want to stir a drink is to prevent the shaking from clouding and/or foaming up the drink. It's all about presentation. You'll want to stir a drink with all clear ingredients (like a Martini or Manhattan) so when it's poured into the cocktail glass, it will come out perfectly clear. If the drink has any cloudy or opaque ingredients (like lemon juice, milk, cream, etc.), it might as well be shaken, since it won't end up clear no matter what you do.

This means you'll need a bar spoon for stirring. Currently in America, we don't have much of a choice. The common bar spoon is a cheap metal spoon with an overly large bowl and a plastic red knob on the end. However, Europeans will find a variety of spoons. Many of them are quite solid with a nice heavy tamping end on them.

Strainer

Once you've stirred or shaken your drink properly, the next step is often to strain it into the glass. The common strainer here is the Hawthorne Strainer. This is a slightly funny looking strainer with a spring around the edge of it. This type of strainer fits really well in the mixing tin of the Boston Shaker, and it is a little tight in the pint glass.

A good Hawthorne Strainer is probably all you need, but you might also want to consider a Julep Strainer. These are harder to find, but they fit nicely within the mixing glass portion of the Boston Shaker and work best when you stir a cocktail instead of shake it.

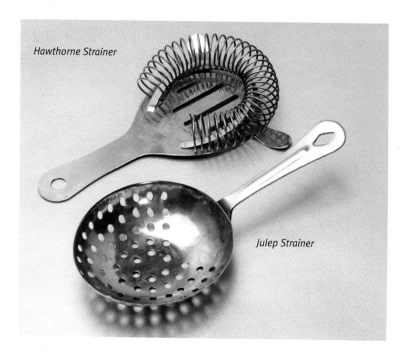

Hawthorne Strainer

Julep Strainer

1950s placemat

Glassware

After taking the time and care to mix your drink properly, you probably want to attractively present it in the proper glassware. Some people get very particular about their glassware and insist that this drink should always be served in that glass. In truth it really doesn't matter that much. While the recent trend has been to carefully match a particular wine with a particular glass that best accentuates its flavors, mixed drinks may be served in any appropriately-sized glass you want to use.

I frankly recommend that you try to have a little fun with your glassware choices. Check out antique shops where you'll find various shapes and sizes of glasses and mix things up a little.

Look through a glassware catalog and you'll find over a dozen types of glasses. However, these are easily divided up into three different categories: stemware, tumblers and mugs.

Let's take a look at some of the more common types of glasses in each of these categories. Later, in the recipe section, you will see the associated icon for a particular glass listed next to the recipe. This indicates which glass is appropriate for that drink.

Stemware

As the name implies, this is a glass with a stem of some sort. Glasses with short stems are often referred to as a footed glass.

Types of stemware include:

 Wine

A typical wineglass is a bulbous glass that slightly narrows at the top to help hold aromas. Small wineglasses with fancy etchings can be fun to use for all sorts of drinks.

 Cocktail (a.k.a. martini)

Cocktails were originally served in small, fancy wine glasses. According to cocktail lore, the common V-shaped glass was popularized at the 1925 Paris Exposition.

The drink most commonly associated with this glass is the Martini. In fact, this association between drink and glass is so strong that many people consider any drink served this way is a Martini, which of course it isn't.

Originally cocktail glasses were around four ounces in size, but over time the tendency to think "bigger means better" made it hard to find a glass less than 9 ounces (270ml). Frankly, that is far too large for a sensible drink. If possible, I recommend trying to find a glass closer to 6 ounces (180ml)—or even less—in size. There's a lot of fun to be had scouring antique stores looking for old cocktail glasses or even champagne coupes, which work quite nicely.

 ## Champagne coupe (a.k.a. saucer)

Looking like a cocktail glass with voluptuous curves, this was once the preferred glass for serving champagne. Often it would have a hollow stem from which a beautiful tower of bubbles emerged. Today the flute glass has replaced the coupe as the glassware of choice for champagne and the coupe is used as a fancy replacement for the cocktail glass. Feel free to use a champagne coupe, which is elegant and reasonably sized, for any drink that might otherwise be served in a V-shaped glass.

 ## Champagne flute (a.k.a. tulip)

This tall and narrow stemmed glass has replaced the coupe as the preferred glass to serve sparkling wine. It provides a beautiful display of bubbles and, because it has less exposed surface area, it keeps the carbonation a bit longer.

It can often be fun to serve sour style cocktails (sidecar, daiquiri, cosmopolitan, etc.) in a flute glass.

Tumblers

A tumbler is any glass without a stem, foot, handle or other such adornment. Usually, but not always, tumblers have straight vertical sides.

Types of tumblers include:

 ## Rocks (a.k.a. lowball, Old Fashioned, bucket)

Short and squat, usually about as high as it is wide, this glass is commonly used for simple drinks served with ice. Normally close to 8 ounces (240ml) in size, you would use this for a Scotch on the Rocks, Old Fashioned or a Gin & Tonic.

 ## Delmonico (a.k.a. fizz, rickey, juice glass)

Rarely referred to these days as a Delmonico glass, these are slightly smaller glasses. They are typically a little taller and narrower than a rocks glass, about 5 ounces (150ml) in size with straight sides.

 ## Highball

Similar to the Delmonico, but taller and wider. Usually holding from 8 to 10 ounces (240 to 360ml), this glass is commonly used for… well… highballs, or drinks which combine a spirit, mixer and ice. In a typical restaurant, this might be the glass used to serve iced water.

Collins (a.k.a. chimney)

Along the same lines as the Delmonico and highball, this glass is taller than a highball and about as wide as a Delmonico. It usually holds from 10 to 12 ounces (300 to 420ml), and would be used for, of course, a Collins, but also for a variety of thirst-quenching summer drinks. These glasses will sometimes have a frosted exterior intended to accentuate the concept of cold and refreshing.

 ## Mugs

As you might expect, a mug is virtually any glass with a handle of some sort. While the glasses listed here are usually (but not always) made from clear glass, mugs are made from a variety of materials: glass, ceramic, metal, wood, etc.

The handle is typically intended to make it easier to drink hot beverages, and so most hot drinks will be served in a mug. There are, however, notable exceptions, such as punch and the Moscow Mule in its iconic copper mug.

1947

Extra Credit

Although we've covered most of what you need to make great cocktails at home, there are a few other tools which might be handy as your skills evolve.

Channel Knife

One of the more common types of cocktail garnish is a lemon twist. The channel knife is a special tool specifically designed to cut those simple little spirals.

To cut a well formed spiral, it's best to use fresh fruit. No matter if it's a lemon, orange, lime or any other citrus you might want to try, spiraling always works best when the fruit is fresh and the skin is nice and tight. Also, always cut the spiral over the drink you'll be serving. As you're cutting a spiral twist, oils from the skin of the citrus will be expelled in a flavorful mist and by cutting over the drink, you'll be making the most use of this flavor.

Vegetable Peeler

A channel knife can cut a very narrow twist, but sometimes you want something a little more substantial. A common vegetable peeler can easily cut a nice solid plank out of most citrus fruits. Remember to cut the twist over the drink. To provide the best possible visual appeal, square the edges of the peel by carefully cleaning it with a knife.

Juicers

Juicer

Many cocktails contain citrus juice. Try to avoid pre-made or commercial juice. Freshly squeezed juices always insure a better drink. If, because of time constraints, you have to squeeze juice ahead of time, try not to let it sit too long. If the juice sits longer than a few hours, it will start to get bitter instead of sour.

There are a wide variety of juicers available. The best ones for cocktails will be those that will expel some of the essential oils from the skin of the fruit into the juice. Mexican Juicers do a good job of this because they essentially turn the fruit inside out as they squeeze out its juices. Their downside is that they're a little messy.

Muddler

The traditional muddler often looks like a miniature baseball bat. It's used much the same way a mortar and pestle are. The muddler is the pestle and the mixing glass is the mortar.

You can use a muddler for crushing sugar cubes, rendering juice from a quartered lime or crushing mint leaves and other herbs to extract their essences. Remember, you shouldn't be too aggressive, especially when herbs are involved. If you grind mint leaves too much, you'll start to extract some of the bitter enzymes they contain instead of just the fresh mint flavor.

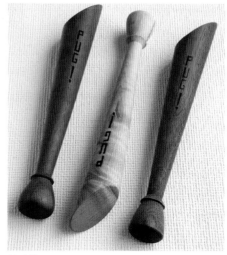

Muddlers

Also, be careful of the Seattle Muddle, which is dropping some citrus wedges in a glass, topping it with ice, then muddling through the ice with the mistaken impression that you are getting some great juice. Instead, you are fighting through the ice and barely touching the wedges. A better technique is to dry muddle (muddle without ice) or, better yet, muddle with a little granulated sugar if the recipe calls for it. The sugar will abrade the skin of the citrus and extract more of its oils.

Knife

From slicing citrus to cutting the foils off wine bottles, good knifes will have multiple uses behind the bar.

It's usually best to have a couple different sizes. While a paring knife will satisfy most of your needs, a chef's knife, for example, is better for cutting larger fruit.

Come to think of it, a cutting board wouldn't be a bad idea either.

Cocktail Pitcher

As previously mentioned, not all cocktails are shaken. While you can use the mixing glass portion of a Boston Shaker for stirring your cocktails, I personally prefer a cocktail pitcher for this. Today, most are made of glass and come with a handle and a formed spout. The spout should be designed to automatically hold back the ice or you'll need to use your hawthorne or julep strainer to help hold back the ice as you pour.

My favorite cocktail pitchers have a metal rim around the top with a built-in strainer. To the best of my knowledge, nobody is making these anymore. Look for them in antique shops or online auctions.

Mesh Strainer

A mesh strainer is used to double-strain a drink. We may be getting a little fussy here, but many bars will choose to fine strain some cocktails to keep any pulp or ice shards from getting into the glasses. For most purposes, a small fine hand-strainer will do the job nicely.

Double-straining

Stocking Your Home Bar

If you're interested in setting up a home bar, you've probably seen, if not looked for, a comprehensive shopping list of the general purpose spirits, cordials, mixers and flavorings that you'll need to make many of the drinks in this or any other cocktail recipe book.

Frankly, this approach is fraught with problems. For one thing, it can be very expensive, and the cost may drive you to settle for cheaper and often inferior products. For another thing, you can end up with lots of products you never actually use.

Fortunately, there's an excellent solution to these problems.

Rather than starting with a shopping list of products to buy, why not select a cocktail you want to make. Look up the recipe for that cocktail, and pick up just the products you need for that one drink. Simple, straightforward and effective.

For the next week or so, make that drink over and over again. Reach a point where you really understand what each ingredient is doing to the drink, and how the way you prepare it comes into play. Play around with the recipe a little bit. Perhaps look up a few alternate recipes and see how the drink is changed.

In effect, you want to own this drink. You want to fully understand what defines the drink and allows it to strut its stuff. Then, select another drink and start the whole process all over again.

Eventually, you will start to run out of one product or another. Before you reach empty, go buy a replacement, but whatever you do, don't buy the same brand. By selecting another brand, you can do a taste test to determine your preference. In this way you will discover the products you personally like best for the cocktails you make the most.

There are multiple benefits from this approach. First, you're going to spend a lot less on your first liquor store run. Second, you're going to have a tighter focus on what you're trying to achieve. Third, after a couple of months, you're going to have a well stocked liquor cabinet. And finally, you're going to know how to make a great cocktail with every single product in your cabinet.

Mixology 101

We've now covered a lot of the basic material and it's time to look at some of the terminology, techniques and secrets that every good bartender should know. Some of these will simply add to your knowledge, but many will allow you to make far better cocktails than you might otherwise.

Balance

To me, the most essential secret to great cocktails involves balance. Any drink served should strike a careful balance among all the flavors contained. It shouldn't taste boozy, nor should it be watery. Sweet ingredients shouldn't overwhelm everything else. Likewise, a drink that's too sour will be sipped and quickly put down. Strive to make the entire drink enchanting and tasteful, all the way to the last sip.

Ingredients

Use quality ingredients if you want to make a quality cocktail. Keep comparing different products to discover which ingredients work best for the drinks you are making. For a less expensive way to compare spirits, look for mini-bottles at your local liquor store.

Measuring

Often you'll see bartenders pour ingredients without seeming to measure. In fact, they have taught themselves to do this and, with practice, they're able to get amazingly close to the correct measurements.

However, when making cocktails, it's essential to measure as accurately as possible. Even when ingredients are measured in increments as small as $\frac{1}{4}$ ounce (7ml), you'll soon realize that the slightest variation will change the flavor of the drink you are making. So take the time to carefully and accurately measure each ingredient you are using.

Ice

It's easy to overlook an ingredient as important as ice, but we shouldn't. Ice plays an extremely important role in any mixed drink. Not only is it providing such a signature component as the chill to the drink, it also is providing an important hidden ingredient in the form of water.

As ice chills, it also melts, and as it melts, it releases water into the drink. Don't assume that water is a bad thing because it will dilute the drink. The amount of alcohol in the drink doesn't decrease as ice melts in the glass. What really happens is the sharp bite of the alcohol gets tamed by the gentle smoothness of water. This is crucial for the balance we are striving for.

Some people will store their alcohol in a freezer to guarantee they can make the coldest drinks possible. Unfortunately, this hurts the overall quality of a drink because ice won't melt as fast in ice cold spirits. Thus, the proper amount of water won't get added, and the drink will end up being overly hot with alcohol. If you want a good drink, you should be looking for the balance that the water will add.

So, keep your booze out of the freezer, and keep your ice cold, clean and in good supply.

Shaking Versus Stirring

We've established that the purpose of both shaking and stirring is essentially the same, to chill the drink down rapidly and to that end, both do an equally great job of it. There are, however, slight differences between the two. Stirring takes longer to chill the drink than shaking, but, in the end, the same amount of water gets released into the drink. This might make you feel that shaking is the preferred way to mix a cocktail. Shaking, however, will agitate the drink more and infuse it with air bubbles. This will make the drink cloudy, and often leave a less than desirable foam on top. Stirring, on the other hand, will leave the drink almost crystal clear.

So which should you use, and when? There's one basic rule of thumb which we touched upon earlier, but it's worth repeating. If the drink is made from all clear ingredients, it should be stirred in order to preserve the clarity. On the other hand, if the drink includes milk, cream, an opaque or cloudy ingredient or eggs, it should be shaken since nothing you do will make it clear.

Chilled Glassware

Cocktails should be served well chilled. Pouring a cold liquid into a room temperature glass, however, will quickly start warming the drink as the thermal dynamics between the glass and the liquid strive to balance out.

Chilling the glasses first is an important step in making a great cocktail. The easiest way to do this is to store your glasses in the freezer. At home, however, you may not be able to find that much room in your freezer. Many bars, in fact, have dedicated refrigerators specifically for this purpose.

An easy way to chill your glasses at home is to place some cracked ice in the glass and fill the glass with water. Do this before you start making your drink so it has plenty of time to chill. Before pouring your drink into the glass, make sure you pour the melted water out. Be a little sloppy about it. If you allow the chilled water to spread down the outside of the glass, it will help chill that side as well.

Garnishes

Adding a beautiful garnish to a cocktail is the final step in making a great drink. There are a variety of common garnishes. These include citrus twists or wedges, cherries, olives, mint, pineapple, even edible flowers and little paper umbrellas. There really isn't much limiting what you can use for a garnish, but you should always be careful to select garnishes appropriate for the cocktail and/or the situation.

Often a simple twist of lemon peel can be the best and easiest way to garnish a drink. There is, however, a right way to do this so that it provides the most effective transformation to the drink.

Using a channel knife or vegetable peeler, you want to cut the twist over the drink. This allows oils from the skin to be expelled over the drink and add some additional flavorings to accent the drink.

In addition, you may want to rub the twist around the edge of the glass before dropping it in. This will add additional oils to the glass edge, which will further accentuate the drink with each sip. Be sure to rub the colored side of the peel against the glass and not the pithy white. The flavorful oils lie on the outside peel.

Rimming

Some cocktails will rely on rimming a glass with some sort of flavoring. For a Margarita this is often salt, for a Lemon Drop it is usually sugar and for a Bloody Mary it can be a combination of salt, chili powder and, perhaps, some dried herbs.

You can buy a foam pad to moisten the glass with as well as special containers to hold the sugar and salt. Frankly, these work best only in bars where speed is more important than quality.

The best way to rim a glass is to first moisten the rim of the glass with something that will help the rimming spice stick. A quick method is to take a wedge of lemon or lime, cut a slot in the fruit, and, inserting the rim into the slot, rub it around the edge of the glass. If a rim is to be sugared, you can dip the rim in a little plate of simple syrup.

By putting your rimming material in the outer ring of a tea saucer, you can easily invert the glass into the saucer and the salt, sugar, or spice will stick reasonably well. A better way, however, one which will rim only the outside of the drink, is to use a spoon to cascade the rimming material on the outside of the glass. In this way you can create a nice wide, not to mention very dramatic, rim.

When rimming with sugar, keep in mind that moisture on the outside of the glass will cause the sugar to migrate down the glass, forming a messy sticky film. Sugared rims are best done an hour or so before the glass is to be used, giving the water a chance to dry. This will also harden the sugar into a nice shell and keep your fingers from getting too sticky.

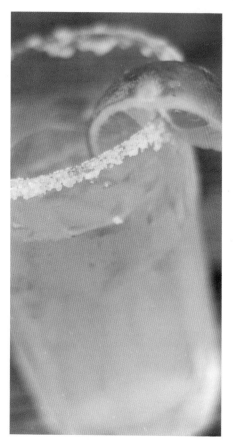

Nothing is written in stone

As you continue learning about making cocktails and mixed drinks, you will encounter recipes that differ or contradict one another. This is natural, and you shouldn't let it confuse you. Just as there are many different ways to make something as common as hash browns, so you'll find different ways have come about to make different drinks. Some recipes and methods are better than others. When you encounter a different approach, take the time to see how it differs from what you're used to and determine for yourself how it might change the drink. You might even experiment a little on your own, and see if you can improve upon some of the recipes and methods found here.

the twister
Jigger Smirnoff Vodka. Add ice and fill glass with 7-Up. Garnish with twist of lemon.

vodka martini
4 parts Smirnoff Vodka, 1 part Dry Vermouth with ice in mixing glass, stir well. Strain into cocktail glass. Garnish with lemon peel, pearl onion or olive.

the screwdriver
Jigger Smirnoff Vodka in highball glass with ice. Fill with orange juice and stir.

vodka'n tonic
Jigger Smirnoff Vodka in highball glass with ice. Fill with quinine water, garnish with slice of lemon or lime.

bloody mary
Jigger Smirnoff Vodka, 3 oz. heavy tomato juice, ½ oz. fresh lemon juice, 4 drops Worcestershire Sauce, 1 dash salt, 1 dash pepper. Shake well with cracked ice and serve.

vodka on the rocks
Just pour Smirnoff Vodka over ice cubes in an Old-Fashioned glass or small tumbler. Add a twist of lemon peel and serve.

vodka collins
Jigger Smirnoff Vodka, 1 oz. lemon juice, 1½ teaspoon powdered sugar. Add ice and shake well. Fill 12 oz. glass with charged water. Garnish with cherry and slice of lemon.

re ways than one . . . *Smirnoff* VODKA

1960s

The Base Spirits

At the core of the bartender's stash of ingredients is what is commonly referred to as the base spirits. Simply defined, there are six base spirits: brandy, gin, rum, tequila, vodka and whiskey. Usually, but not always, one of these will be the foundation of any mixed drink or cocktail.

Brandy

Brandy is the classification given to any spirit which is based on fruit. While almost any fruit can be used to make a brandy, grapes are the most common. A bottle simply labeled as brandy is most likely made from a distilled wine. Brandy from other fruits will be labeled as Cherry Brandy, Peach Brandy or whatever is appropriate. There are some fruit brandies which have taken on specific names, such as calvados for apple brandy made in Normandy, applejack for apple brandy made in America, Kirsch or Kirshwasser for cherry brandy, Slivovitz for plum brandy, etc.

Brandy from fruit other than grapes is also often referred to as *eau de vie*, which translates from the French as *water of life*. An *eau de vie* will almost always be clear since traditionally it's never aged.

Cognac and Armagnac

To say that cognac and armagnac are nothing more than brandies is both being truthful and disrespectful at the same time. A brandy can only be labeled cognac or armagnac if it is made in those specific regions of France, following specific methods and processes.

Today, cognac is the more popular of the two, a result of geography more than anything else. The Cognac region of France has an easier access to the sea and therefore distribution than its land-locked cousin does.

Very Superior Old Pale

You will often see labeling such as VS (Very Superior), VSOP (Very Superior Old Pale) and XO (Extra Old) on both armagnac and cognac. Essentially VS is a very young brandy, VSOP is slightly older and XO is slightly older than that. It is difficult to make quality judgments between different brands solely on their label designation. A VSOP from one brand can often be better than an XO from another.

Rum

Rum is a distilled product made from sugar in sugar cane juice, sugar syrup or molasses. The process is relatively simple, even more so than most other spirits, since there isn't any need for special processing to prepare the sugars to feed the yeasts that will in turn produce the alcohol.

Sugar Cane

Modern rum production is centered in the Caribbean Islands since they are one of the major producers of sugar cane in the world.

One by-product of refining sugar is molasses. Initially, molasses was seen as a waste product, but soon somebody had the idea of fermenting the molasses to see what could be made from it. This was the beginning of rum.

Whiskey

Simply put, whiskey is a product distilled from grain. Whiskey gets its name from *uisgebeatha* (Irish) and *uisgebaugh* (Scottish), both of which translate as *water of life*. The names, being somewhat difficult for non-native speakers to pronounce, were eventually simplified to *whiskey*.

To *e* or not to *e*

Traditionally you use whiskey when you refer to Irish or American whiskey. And you use whisky when you refer to Scotch or Canadian whisky. Precisely why this came about is debatable, and it isn't without its exceptions. Here in America, both Maker's Mark and George Dickle label their products as whisky.

Blended Whiskies

As the name implies, this is a whiskey made from a blending of different whiskies.

Irish Whiskey

Irish whiskey is made from malted barley. Since the grains are kept from coming into contact with the smoke from whatever heat source is used, Irish whiskey won't have the smoky character of a Scotch whisky.

Scotch Whisky

The major difference between Irish whiskey and Scotch whisky is that during the Scottish malting process the germinated barley is allowed to be touched by the smoke from the peat fires used to dry the grain out. This produces that unique smoky flavor found, to a certain degree, in all Scotch whisky.

There may be some confusion about the term *single malt* in reference to Scotch whisky. Technically this isn't a term referring to a Scotch made from a single malt, but is, in fact, two terms. Single means that it is a scotch from a single distillery, and malt means that it is only made from malted barley without any neutral grain spirits added. On the other hand, a blended Scotch is a whisky made by blending whiskies from different distilleries.

American Whiskey

American whiskies are essentially broken down into three main categories: rye, bourbon and blended.

American Rye Whiskey

The first Irish and Scottish immigrants to America continued the distilling practices learned back home. However, they had to make do with whatever they found available here. So, instead of using the traditional barley, they relied on other grains to make their mash. Rye quickly became the grain of choice, and many early American whiskies were made from rye. Rye whiskey dominated the market until Prohibition.

Barley

American Bourbon Whiskey

As the country expanded, settlers once again had to adjust to the grains available for fermentation. Away from the east, corn was the staple and whiskey was made from corn mixed with wheat, rye and other grains.

Kentucky rapidly became a state known for its whiskey. Distilleries in Kentucky and throughout the Midwest made good use of the Mississippi River to distribute their product as far south as New Orleans. There was one problem, however. Corn was harvested in the fall, and the Mississippi wouldn't be high enough for serious boat traffic until the spring. This meant that whiskey had to sit around in barrels for almost half a year before it could be delivered.

It soon became apparent that this extra time in the barrels produced a new whiskey that was a lot smoother than any before. Bourbon County, Kentucky became associated with this whiskey and people were soon asking specifically for bourbon whiskey.

Gin

Most spirits are defined by the main component of their fermented base. Gin, however, is defined by what is added during the distillation process.

Making Gin

As most people know, dried juniper berries are the defining ingredient in gin. The other ingredients are the choice of the distillery. Things like lemon peel, orange peel, anise, orris root, angelica root, cardamom, coriander, licorice root, cinnamon, almond, lavender and cassia are some of the more common ingredients. Some gins include rose petals, cucumber, mint, dried apples and even hops.

Gin starts out with a neutral spirit, which is almost, but not quite, pure alcohol. Carefully chosen botanicals are then added. The mixture is soaked for a time and then distilled again. The resulting spirit includes many flavor components of the macerated botanicals.

Bathtub Gin

During Prohibition, gin got a bit of a bum rap. Since gin is basically alcohol with added flavorings, gangster entrepreneurs entered into the illegal manufacturing of gin in great numbers. They would often take high-proof grain alcohol, add flavor concentrates to it, water it down and present it as gin. This concoction earned the nickname bathtub gin. There are, of course, various problems with this approach. It's about the same as making wine by simply adding grape juice to alcohol.

The Cocktailian Spirit

Arguably, gin is one of the best spirits to make cocktails. Unfortunately, it also appears that most drinkers tend to shy away from it. I think that the reason for this is quite simple. All of the base spirits have an ongoing tradition of being taken straight. It isn't uncommon to take shots or snifters of brandy, rum, whiskey, tequila or vodka. However, you never hear of someone asking for a snifter or shot of gin. The reason is quite simple: gin really isn't intended to be drunk by itself. It not only needs to be mixed with other flavors, but actually shines when done properly. Most experienced bartenders love to work with gin because it provides an exciting palate of flavors to complement other ingredients.

Tequila

Tequila starts out as the fermented sap of the agave plant which is then distilled. That's almost the whole story, but not quite.

Mescal

Frankly, labeling this section *tequila* is like labeling the brandy section *cognac*. Instead we should have named this section *mescal* (mezcal in Spanish), which is the name applied to any spirit made from the fermented sap of the agave plant. In order to be labeled tequila, the mescal needs to be made in the Jalisco region of Mexico, and it has to be made from at least 51% blue agave. Premium producers will use 100% blue agave, and will proudly state so on their label.

Tequila Styles

When buying tequila, you will find several different styles. The three main styles are Blanco (Silver), Reposado (Rested) and Añejo (Aged).

Blanco tequila is unaged tequila. It has a bright vegetal flavor since it hasn't spent any time in barrels to mellow its flavors. Reposado tequila has been aged in oak barrels for at least two months, but not more than a year. This short time in oak will mellow the flavor slightly and add a little golden color to it. Añejo refers to tequila aged in oak barrels for more than a year but less than three. This extended time in oak will greatly mature the flavors, bringing an almost brandy-like flavor to the tequila.

There are some other important designations for tequila. One most commonly seen is *Gold*. This refers to an unaged tequila which has been colored and flavored--usually with caramel-- in order to make it look and taste like an aged tequila. Most gold tequilas are also what is referred to as *mixto* tequilas. These aren't made from 100% blue agave and, in most cases, aren't even made from 100% agave. Instead some sugar is added to the agave piña to boost the available sugars for the fermentation process.

I generally prefer to use a silver tequila

in cocktails. It provides a very distinctive tequila flavor which, when combined well with other ingredients, is an excellent way to celebrate this spirit.

While mescal and tequila have been produced in Mexico since the 1500s, they weren't recognized ingredients for cocktails or mixed drinks until Prohibition, a time period when Americans were looking both north and south for replacements for their beloved American whiskey.

Vodka

Original vodkas bore little similarity to what we think of as vodka today. In fact, vodka would have been a generic term used to refer to any distilled spirit, regardless of what it was distilled from or what it tasted like. As distillation techniques gradually improved, focus was paid to clarifying the spirit. When column distillation finally came onto the scene, vodka manufacturing was quickly revolutionized.

Making Vodka

Unlike brandy, rum, tequila or whiskey, vodka can be made from anything fermentable. Most people think of vodka as being made with potatoes, but most vodka is made from grain, which is far more cost effective. However, vodka is also made from grapes and sugar. It has even been made from milk!

Distilleries manufacturing vodka have great advantages over those making other spirits. Unlike most spirits, vodka can be created anywhere, out of anything and, most importantly, can be bottled immediately after distillation without the added time and expense of barrel aging.

Training Wheels

Used in cocktails, vodka can be seen as the liquid equivalent of training wheels. To those just discovering the joys of cocktails and mixed drinks, the unfamiliar and complex flavors of spirits like gin, whiskey and tequila can sometimes be a little too jarring. On the other hand, vodka has the bite of alcohol without the complexity of other flavors that might puzzle new drinkers. Further, you can easily add vodka to almost any otherwise non-alcoholic drink, and it suddenly becomes an adult beverage.

Other Cocktail Ingredients

The Bartender's Pantry

Spirits are only the starting point for making a cocktail or mixed drink. It's what you add to that spirit which turns it into a cocktail and defines its culinary identity.

Originally, the palate of ingredients added to various drinks was relatively limited. Some ingredients just didn't exist yet, but many hadn't been embraced yet by the bartenders of the day.

Initially, simple sweeteners and citrus juices were the stock of the day, along with a variety of fruits and berries used as garnishes, sometimes with abandon.

Over time, additional ingredients made their ways into various drinks, and with each new addition, the culinary potentials of the drinks would take radical leaps forward. It's as if a cook who had been limited to onions, potatoes and chicken suddenly discovered the wonders of salt, cumin and butter. That's when the genie finally gets released from the bottle.

Let's take a quick look at some ingredients used to prepare the cocktail recipes included here.

Cordials and Syrups

Sweeteners have long played a big roll in mixed drinks. Initially used as a way to mask unwanted flavors, they gradually and rightfully were seen as a major element in the all important balancing act that can make these drinks magical.

The essence of whatever drink you are having or making is the balance of flavors. Drinks which are overly sweet or sour are mere pretenders, hoping that screaming their flavors loudly will prevent people from recognizing that there isn't any craftsmanship behind them.

The first sweeteners--most likely, fruits and berries--added their natural sweetness, flavors and tartness to various drinks. When sugar became more readily available, it quickly supplanted other sweeteners as the sweetener of choice. This was an easy decision because sugar stored for a long time and it added only sweetness to the equation, thus allowing its effect on the drink to be controlled better.

Also, the availability of sugar led to an increased production of cordials and flavored syrups whose gains in popularity were aided by their cheaper prices.

In the mid-1800s, sweeteners in addition to sugar included orgeat syrup (a sweet syrup made from barley and later almonds prepared with an extract of orange flowers and sugar), maraschino liqueur (made using the marascas cherry), curaçao a.k.a curaçoa (made using the peel of sour oranges) and various berry syrups. Over time, the landscape expanded until today, there are hundreds of possible choices for sweetening a drink.

Simple Syrup

A first encounter with simple syrup as an ingredient in a cocktail recipe usually causes a certain level of confusion. To complicate matters, it's an unlikely product to be found at a liquor or grocery store.

Simple syrup is exactly what the name says, simple. It's easy to make by dissolving sugar in water. The specific ratios vary from person to person. Some prefer using equal amounts by volume of water and sugar, while others use twice as much sugar as water. The 2-to-1 version is often referred to as rich simple syrup.

Sugar is dissolved in water in one of two ways. The most traditional method is to bring the water to a simmer and then stir in the sugar until it dissolves. Allow it to cool, and bottle it. You can also combine the sugar and water in a bottle, close it tight, shake it until it's completely dissolved and then shake it a little more for good measure.

Either way, if the syrup is stored at room temperature for more than a day, add about an ounce of vodka per quart to prevent mold from accumulating.

Other Syrups

To go from a simple syrup made from sugar and water, it is easy to move into various flavored syrups. Grenadine is just simple syrup in which you have simmered pomegranate seeds for a while in order to allow them to impart their flavors. Besides a variety of syrups made from various fruits, berries, and sometimes even spices, you will occasionally encounter orgeat (an almond flavored syrup) or falernum (an almond syrup with the addition of clove, ginger, lime, and a few other spices). With the popularity of coffee shops these days, you can often find a variety of flavors available in the coffee sections of many supermarkets.

Cordials, Liqueurs and Crèmes

You will often see the terms cordial and liqueur used interchangeably. Each refers to a sweet and usually alcoholic beverage with a fruit, herb or sometimes spice flavor. To provide some level of separation, some countries put specific requirements on each.

Liqueurs

There are a large number of cordials available, and they are quite popular in a wide range of mixed drinks. There are two specific types of cordials which I want to quickly touch upon, one because it is so popular that there are a variety of confusing products, and the other because it is rather uncommon, but deserves to be better understood.

Curaçao and Other Orange Cordials

It's likely that the most popular sweet cordial flavor in cocktails is orange. It goes by many names and comes in several forms. One of the first was curaçao, today often called orange curaçao. It's a relatively simple orange flavored liqueur. Originally curaçao used brandy as its base spirit, but now it generally uses a neutral grain spirit. Triple sec evolved in the early 1800s as a cleaner, more refined version of orange curaçao.

Most brands of both curaçao and triple sec are relatively inexpensive, and their quality is usually reflected in their price. If you're looking for premium brands, you'll want to pick up Grand Marnier (which has a brandy base) to use as your orange curaçao and Cointreau (which has a neutral grain spirit base) to use for recipes calling for triple sec.

When looking for curaçao, you will often find it in clear, orange and blue varieties. Given that there's no difference in flavor, I always recommend either the clear or orange variety since the blue will only work in cocktails intentionally meant to be blue (in other words very few).

Maraschino Liqueur

Once commonly used in a variety of cocktails, maraschino liqueur gradually disappeared as the cocktails which used it fell into obscurity. With the classic cocktail resurgence, maraschino liqueur is seeing a radical and well deserved comeback. Like curaçao, it is essentially a sweet fruit liqueur flavored, as the name implies, from cherries. Its character is less sweet but more complex than curaçao since the flavor comes not just from the fruit but the seeds as well. This results in a slightly diverse set of flavors that seem to provide hints of chocolate, vanilla and almonds.

Maraschino liqueur should not be confused with modern maraschino cherries. There is no similarity between the two, and heaven help the bartender who substitutes the juice from a jar of maraschino cherries for maraschino liqueur in a cocktail.

Aromatized Wines

Wines have a much older history than spirits. Many of the oldest wines probably have more in common with vermouth than with modern wines.

Aromatized wines

Aromatized wines are the result of adding various herbs and botanicals to a wine. It's also common to add some brandy or other spirit, which allows them to be called *fortified* wines. These additions result in a wine that is less fragile then normal, one that will travel better since it isn't as susceptible to going bad soon after opening. The added alcohol will forestall the onset of oxidation for a while and the botanicals will help mask the taste of wine going bad.

This is not to say that an aromatized wine is shelf stable. When possible you should store an open bottle in the refrigerator or plan to use it within a week. After that time, not only will the flavor start to deteriorate, but wine left out too long will begin tossing sediments that are visible as black or white specks in your drink.

While vermouth (both sweet, and dry) is perhaps the most well known of the aromatized/fortified wines, other popular products include Dubonnet and Lillet.

Bitters

Bitters used in a cocktail can come in two different varieties. Cocktail bitters, meant to be used sparingly, usually comes in a very small bottle with a dasher top. Digestive bitters, which are used in amounts you can actually measure, may be drunk straight. The line between the two can get a little hazy.

Cocktail Bitters

Because we've mentioned cocktail bitters so frequently, you've probably realized how important we feel they are to the cocktail. Unfortunately, they are often slighted by the majority of bartenders. Once there were dozens of different cocktail bitters available to the classically trained bartender. Today, depending on how you count them, you'll find just over a dozen varieties. Still, the situation is a lot better than it was just a few years ago.

Bitters are essentially a combination of multiple herbs and spices, which are soaked in alcohol to extract very concentrated flavors before bottling. They are usually alcoholic and are not normally intended to be taken straight. Their flavor is very intense, but, when used in small dashes, they aromatize a cocktail and support and enhance its flavors.

Angostura bitters is far and away the most popular cocktail bitters, but Peychaud's bitters is almost as old a brand and is being seen much more lately. Other brands include a variety of different styles from Fee Brothers, Regan's Orange Bitters #6, The Bitter Truth, and even many which are now being made by various bartenders themselves.

Digestive Bitters

Digestive Bitters can often be difficult to classify since some may be thought of as apéritifs. However, an *apéritif* should stimulate the appetite and be had before a meal while a *digestif* is had following the meal to help settle things down.

I usually consider apéritifs, which include aromatized wines, to be lighter of the two in flavor. On the other hand, a digestif is a complex, almost overpowering, flavor that will put your taste buds down for the count.

Some of the more common brands of what could be considered digestive bitters are Absinthe (Pastis), Bénédictine, Campari, Chartreuse, Fernet Branca, and Jagermeister.

Bitters

Juices

Juices of one sort or another have been a constant component of the mixed drink. Technically and historically, juices don't belong in a cocktail. But, by the later half of the 1800s, that orthodoxy was thrown out the window.
With the potential of an ever-expanding list of available ingredients growing, it was difficult to place too many restrictions on the creativity of the bartenders of the day.

Whenever possible, fresh juices should be seen as the only option for making a quality cocktail. Even if the preparation requires a little extra work and expense, the difference is measurable.

If you don't have time to fresh squeeze your juices for each drink, you can prepare some juice ahead of time. Remember, though, that juices will start going bitter in a short amount of time. You should measure a juice's lifetime in hours not days, and always keep juices well chilled.

Many juices have a fairly aggressive flavor that can quickly overpower a drink if too much is used. For this reason I always highly recommend measuring cocktails carefully. Keep in mind that a recipe calling for something along the lines of "the juice of half a lemon" is imprecise and should always be avoided. The amount of juice from one fruit to the next can vary enough to throw the drink off.

Sour Mix

Finally, I need to say that at no time should you ever consider using sour mix in your cocktails.

Some drinks like the whiskey sour are made with an equal measure of simple syrup and lemon juice. Sour mix was created as a pre-made short cut for mixing those drinks. The idea was to save time by having the mix already at hand. Then, when someone ordered a Whiskey Sour, you had only two bottles to pour from instead of three. Lazy bartenders would then use the same premix to make Daiquiris (which should use lime juice instead of lemon) and then for a Margarita (which should use lime juice instead of lemon and an orange liqueur instead of a plain simple syrup).

Sour Mix suddenly became the hammer, and any drink that needed a sweetening agent and a souring agent of any sort was suddenly seen as the nail. Add commercialization to the mix, and instead of a mix of simple syrup and lemon juice, sour mix is being made from high fructose corn syrup, citric acid and a variety of additional flavorings, stabilizers and preservatives.

The Classic Cocktails

Before rattling off a couple hundred cocktail recipes, let's take a look at a few of the basics. These will provide the foundation upon which most of the other drinks you're likely to make are based. By looking at these in detail, you'll be better prepared to tackle recipes that come with few specifics on preparation.

All of these foundation recipes are for drinks that are relatively common. In some cases the presentation differs from what might be served by bartenders today. In these cases I'll explain the differences and why they exist.

Select a recipe and pick up the necessary ingredients. I'd recommend spending at least a week on each of the drinks in this section and really mastering it. As you master each of these recipes, I'd like to suggest you do a little research. Check alternate recipes online or in other books. Try some of the variations to determine your preferences and always ask yourself, "Why is this better than that?"

Nothing is written in stone. This means that the recipes listed here shouldn't be seen as *the* recipe for any particular drink any more then the recipe for tomato soup you might find in a cookbook should be thought of as the only way tomato soup should be made. It's my intent, however, for you to enjoy every recipe and learn how to make the best cocktails possible.

Sidecar

- 2 ounces (60ml) brandy (cognac)
- 1 ounce (30ml) Cointreau
- ½ ounce (15ml) lemon juice

Shake with ice.

Strain into cocktail glass.

Someone new to cocktails may find that many have a flavor profile that's too jarring. The martini is one of the quintessential cocktails, but neophytes may think you're asking them to drink a shot of Tabasco.

This version of the sidecar is a good place to begin to show what real cocktails are all about. I use the word *version* since this isn't the original recipe, nor is likely to be what you'd be served in most bars today.

When it first appeared in print, the sidecar was equal parts cognac, Cointreau and lemon juice. Frankly, I find that this makes a drink that's far too sour for the palate. The first few sips might be fine, but, by the time you get to the end, you're ready to move on to something else.

Beware of the modern Sidecar. It's often just brandy and sour mix, a sad drink by any measure.

The Sidecar was one of the first cocktails that I taught myself. I went through a variety of recipes before settling on this one. I feel that the ratios presented here, specifically using Cointreau and fresh lemon juice, result in a drink that is smooth as velvet and, when you reach the end, you wish you had made just a little more.

Often this drink is served with a sugared rim, but I find that sugared rims are usually a bad idea. Sugared rims give you a sticky finger problem, but more than that, history is on my side. The original Sidecar recipe didn't call for it either.

For research purposes, you may want to pick up a bottle of triple sec, as well as some bottled lemon juice. Try using triple sec instead of Cointreau and the bottled lemon juice instead of fresh. I think you'll taste the difference.

Also, if you find an online recipe using sour mix, try that as well. I'm confident that this will be a lesson quickly learned.

Daiquiri

- 2 ounces (60ml) light rum
- ¾ ounce (22ml) simple syrup
- ½ ounce (15ml) lime juice

Shake with ice and strain into a cocktail glass.

Garnish with a lime slice.

You'll notice that both the Sidecar and the Daiquiri are made with a base spirit, a sweet ingredient and a sour ingredient. This type of drink in a variety of forms is typically called a sour.

The origin of the Daiquiri is an oft-told story. Around 1896, a man named Jennings Cox mixed a drink combining rum, lime juice, sugar and ice. He served it to friends visiting him in Cuba. The drink was named for a nearby town.

There's nothing remarkable to be found in each individual ingredient. They were all extremely common in Cuba and known for hundreds of years. It's a little more remarkable to think that Mr. Cox suddenly decided to combine them. The story, then, may be apocryphal. It's more likely that this drink was a common refreshment in the area, and Mr. Cox simply introduced his visitors to it.

Most people might think of a Daiquiri as a frozen drink, something that has more in common with a frosty Slushee™ than a refined cocktail. Along Bourbon Street in New Orleans, it's common to see banks of frozen drink machines churning out "Daiquiris" of every flavor imaginable.

The frozen daiquiri is something that should be avoided at all costs. A proper alcoholic drink should never remind you of your childhood. That's just wrong.

Margarita

- 1½ ounce (45ml) tequila
- 1 ounce (30ml) Cointreau
- ½ ounce (15ml) lime juice

Shake with ice.

Strain into an ice-filled Old Fashioned glass or a salt-rimmed margarita glass.

For decades, the Margarita has been the most popular cocktail in the world. Is it because it's so closely associated with Mexican cuisine that it might seem disrespectful not to order a Margarita with your meal? Or is it simply that when properly made, it's an excellent drink?

One of the most common origin stories surrounding the Margarita involves Margarita Sames. It seems that while hosting a party in 1948, Ms. Sames created this special drink to serve to her guests. A nice story and it sounds plausible but, unfortunately, there are enough other stories about the origins of the Margarita that you have to take all of them with a grain of salt.

The Margarita, of course, is also in the sour family. Like the Sidecar and Daiquiri, it combines a spirit with both sweet and sour ingredients to produce a well-balanced drink. Looking back at these recipes, you'll note that each uses slightly different ingredients. It's the ingredients and the flavors they reflect that define each carefully prepared drink.

Just as the making of a frozen drink is often the ruin of the Daiquiri, the Margarita is ruined by the use of a commercial sour mix. Of course, it's hard to ignore the fact that, like the Daiquiri, the Margarita is often also considered to be a frozen drink.

Like the Sidecar, the Margarita is commonly served rimmed, but with salt instead of sugar. Fortunately salt won't give you the same sticky finger effect that an improperly sugared rim will. It will, however, put salt in your drink and a rarely pleasant briny mixture at the bottom of your drink.

When you salt the rim of your Margarita, focus on salting just the outside of the glass without getting salt on the inside. This is easily accomplished by rubbing the rim with a lime wedge and then using a spoon to cascade kosher or pickling salt over the outside of the glass with a spoon.

Cosmopolitan

- 1½ ounce (45ml) citrus vodka
- ½ ounce (15ml) Cointreau
- 1 ounce (30ml) cranberry juice
- ¾ ounce (22ml) lime juice

Shake with ice.

Strain into a cocktail glass.

Garnish with lime wedge.

Possibly the Cosmopolitan is suffering from the popularity it achieved in the 1990s. It's still an extremely common drink to order, but for many it's become rather passé.

This is a shame because, properly made, the Cosmopolitan is not only an excellent cocktail but a worthy member of the same family tree as the Sidecar, Margarita and Daiquiri. Like its cousins, the Cosmopolitan uses a base spirit combined with both sour and sweet ingredients to form a carefully balanced result.

Cosmopolitans start running into problems when shortcuts or cost saving measures are put into play. Cointreau is always preferred to triple sec and fresh squeezed lime juice is critical. The thought of using any form of bottled lime juice or sour mix should never be entertained.

The origins of the Cosmopolitan have been elusive until recently. Noted author and historian Gary Regan believes he recently uncovered the scoop when he was put in touch with a woman named Cheryl Cook. It appears that in 1985 Ms. Cook was the first to mix this drink when she worked at the Strand in South Beach, Miami. She was inspired by the recently introduced Absolut Citron and wanted to create a drink utilizing it. She combined this new vodka with triple sec, Rose's lime juice and just enough cranberry juice to make it "oh so pretty in pink."

The original version of the cocktail evolved into its modern form through the efforts of Dale DeGroff and Toby Cecchini. Both focused on elevating the quality of the drink by using Cointreau instead of triple sec and replacing Rose's lime juice with fresh lime juice. If you want to compare the two versions, please do. I'll think you'll quickly see why the version presented here is the one that quality bars use.

Old Fashioned

- 1 sugar cube (1 teaspoon/5ml)
- 1 teaspoon (5ml) water
- 2 dashes Angostura bitters
- 2 ounces (60ml) American rye or bourbon whiskey

Muddle sugar, water and bitters together until the sugar is mostly dissolved.

Fill glass with ice and then add the whiskey. Stir briefly to chill.

Garnish with a twist of orange peel, and a cherry.

Serve with straws.

According to many stories, the Old Fashioned was invented at the Pendennis Club in Louisville, Kentucky. Unfortunately, history doesn't bare this out. Cocktail researcher David Wondrich uncovered a reference to a drink named the *Old Fashioned* in an 1880 edition of the Chicago Tribune. The Pendennis Club wouldn't open until the next year.

In truth, the Old Fashioned is a "whiskey cocktail made the old fashioned way." By the late 1800s, cocktails had changed so much that somebody from 1810 would no longer recognize one. So, in many ways, the Old Fashioned represents the *original* cocktail.

Unfortunately, this drink is so rarely ordered that most bartenders no longer know how to make it properly. The result tends to be pretty bad.

If you're at all familiar with the Old Fashioned, you may have expected the recipe to mention muddling a slice of orange and cherry with the drink at the start. However, this is a fairly new addition to the drink, and it quite likely marks the beginning of the downfall. The muddled orange may provide an orange flavor that works well with the whiskey, but it also adds bits of citrus pulp to the drink which will clog the straws. Properly adding an orange twist at the end--remember to cut it over the drink--will add a hint of that citrus flavor without the pulp. The muddled cherry only results in a mangled carcass. I'd rather leave the cherry unmolested as a garnish. You might also see bartenders topping off the drink with water or club soda. This is overkill since the water in the recipe makes a simple syrup and should be just enough to do the job. If you'd like, you could use simple syrup and omit the sugar and water all together.

The Classic Martini

- 2½ ounces (75ml) gin
- ¾ ounce (22ml) sweet or dry vermouth
- Dash orange bitters

Stir with ice.

Strain into a cocktail glass.

Garnish with a lemon twist.

Historians continue to debate the origins of the Martini, both who first made it as well as where the name itself comes from. Perhaps less attention should be paid to history and more to making the drink properly.

This recipe may seem strange at first, since it not only includes a lot more vermouth than you've come to expect but it also includes orange bitters. In addition, it doesn't specify which type of vermouth to use. So, I'd like to recommend that you try this first with sweet vermouth instead of the dry you might be used to, since this is the way the drink was originally made.

Any bartender or consumer prior to Prohibition would readily recognize and accept this recipe. Back then many cocktails were made with sweet vermouth, and, if you wanted a variation using dry vermouth instead, you would ask for a *dry* cocktail. Making the recipe above with sweet vermouth would be a true Martini, while making it with dry vermouth would make it a dry Martini.

Like all cocktails, a Martini should represent an artful balance of ingredients. No one ingredient should overshadow another. The modern Martini, however, is often made with merely the vapors of vermouth, and this clearly wouldn't be enough to stand up to the flavor of a good gin. If a Martini is properly made, you shouldn't be able to tell where the gin stops and the vermouth begins. Orange bitters are there to play the roll that bitters always plays in cocktails, to be the accent which blends and enlivens the flavors.

This recipe calls for the drink to be stirred as opposed to shaken. Shaking this drink will result in a cloudy mess while stirring it will give you a crystal clear liquid to pour into a glass.

As for the garnish, on a sweet Martini you can also use a cherry if you wish, and on a dry Martini olives are acceptable, but my preference is to serve them on the side instead.

Manhattan

- 2½ ounces (75ml) American rye or bourbon whiskey
- ¾ ounce (22ml) sweet vermouth
- Dash Angostura bitters

Stir with ice.

Strain into a cocktail glass.

Garnish with a cherry.

Similarities between the Manhattan and the Martini are obvious. Spirit, vermouth, bitters: a simple combination, and one that is elegant and refined as well as bold and assertive.

Like the Martini, a Manhattan is traditionally made with sweet vermouth, and if you wanted it to be made with dry instead, you'd ask for a dry Manhattan. Vermouth cocktails can also be *perfect*, meaning they are made from equal amounts of sweet and dry vermouth. This is a variation worth trying as you acquaint yourself with the Manhattan and the Martini.

It should come as no surprise that the Manhattan almost certainly originated in New York City. More precise details, however, are difficult to nail down. The first recorded appearances are in the early 1880s, and many accounts indicate that it was created for a banquet hosted by Jennie Jerome, Winston Churchill's mother, at the Manhattan Club. The banquet celebrated Samuel Tilden's election as governor. The story doesn't hold up, however, since the inaugural celebrations coincided with the precise time Jennie Jerome was giving birth to her famous son in Oxfordshire, England.

The traditional Martini suffered terribly following Prohibition, but the Manhattan wasn't inflicted with a similar fate. You may occasionally encounter a bartender who will leave out the bitters, but, for the most part, the recipe is intact and the drink recognizable. The worst, and very common, offense is that bartenders will shake their Manhattans instead of stirring them. This not only results in a cloudy drink but unappetizing debris of foam across the top. Like a Martini, the Manhattan should always be stirred.

Bloody Mary

- 1½ ounce (45ml) vodka
- 3 ounces (90ml) tomato juice
- ½ ounce (15ml) lemon juice
- Worcestershire sauce to taste
- Tabasco sauce to taste
- Black pepper to taste
- Celery salt to taste

Roll with ice until properly chilled, and then pour into a tall glass.

Garnish with a celery stalk and a wedge of lemon.

Let's start off by defining what *roll* means. Using a normal Boston Shaker, pour the ingredients from the mixing tin to the mixing glass and back again. This will mix and chill the ingredients well without causing the tomato juice to break down and get thin.

It's said that George Jessel came up with a drink combining equal parts vodka and tomato juice and called it a Bloody Mary. However, around 1920, Fernand "Pete" Petiot of Harry's New York Bar in Paris turned Jessel's drink into the drink we know today by adding salt, pepper and Worcestershire sauce.

When Prohibition ended, the St. Regis Hotel in New York hired

Fernand away from Harry's in Paris, and he brought his Bloody Mary with him. Two changes were made to it, however. Since vodka wasn't widely available in the U.S., gin was used instead. Also, the owners of the St. Regis thought Bloody Mary was too crude of a name, so they renamed it the Red Snapper.

The Bloody Mary is a drink that demands a personalized recipe from one bar to the next. It can be considered the meatloaf of cocktails, since a variety of different flavors and ingredients can be combined together. As long as you keep within broad generalities, everybody still accepts it as meatloaf or, in this case, a Bloody Mary.

Many people like to add to, or replace, the Tabasco sauce with horseradish or wasabi. You can also use any one of hundreds of hot sauces available. For a little extra depth, I like to add a tablespoon of chili powder (dried chilies ground to a powder). Various other seasoning options are almost limitless.

Garnishes also allow variety and creativity. Pickled string beans, asparagus spears, olives, scallions or shrimp are just a few ideas you can use.

Mai Tai

- 1 ounce (30ml) light rum
- 1 ounce (30ml) gold rum
- ½ ounce (15ml) orange curaçao
- ½ ounce (15ml) orgeat (almond syrup)
- ½ ounce (15ml) lime juice
- ½ ounce (15ml) dark rum (optional)

Shake all but the dark rum with ice.

Strain into an ice-filled rocks glass.

Top with the dark rum if you wish, then garnish with a maraschino cherry.

The Mai Tai is the most well-known drink to come out of the Tiki era, which started in the 1930s and then began to run out of steam in the 1970s.

At the beginning of the Tiki era, there was an enforced veil of secrecy wrapped around most of the exotic drinks served at Polynesian-inspired restaurants. Because these restaurants wanted to keep these drinks unique to their venue, they guarded their recipes as if they were the crown jewels, which in some respect they were. Secrecy went to such an extreme that even the bartenders didn't know the actual recipes they were making.

Recipes would list, for example, 1/2 ounce syrup #2," without a clue as to what the ingredient really was.

This was, of course, a problem for the consumer. After enjoying a wonderful drink like the Mai Tai at Trader Vic's, he or she might ask for a Mai Tai at another restaurant. The bartender, of course, wouldn't know what it was. But a shrewd bartender might ask the customer a few questions about the drink to see if he or she could approximate it. If the result met with the customer's approval, the recipe would be used to satisfy other requests. This has left us with some recipes listing pineapple juice, grenadine, falernum, orange juice or various other ingredients that should never be used making this drink.

The Mai Tai was invented in 1944 by Victor "Trader Vic" Bergeron. He mixed Jamaican rum, juice from a fresh lime, a few dashes of orange curaçao syrup, some French orgeat and rock candy syrup. According to Trader Vic history, the drink was served to some friends from Tahiti, who promptly proclaimed "*Mai Tai, Roa Ae*!" which in Tahitian means "Out of this world, the best!"

CLASSIC COCKTAILS

The Recipes

INTRODUCTION

This section contains a very personal collection of recipes that I think you will enjoy. The intent is not to list every conceivable drink recipe but rather represent the best a cocktail or mixed drink has to offer.

Where appropriate, I've included additional information to help you better understand how to make a drink. Sometimes the information will convey the history surrounding a particular drink.

Some of the drinks included have been created by myself or other bartenders around the world, and so you may not be familiar with them. In those cases I've listed who created the drink, when, and usually a comment from the originator providing details on his or her inspiration.

As you read through these recipes, keep in mind that none of them should be seen as the definitive recipe for that drink, just the recipe that I feel represents how its ingredients can be best combined for maximum flavor. You will certainly encounter other recipes for the same drink, which will vary slightly from what you find here. In such cases it can be highly educational to try the other recipes to discover which variation you prefer.

Old fashioned barware

The specific measurements are recommendations, and you should feel free to adjust the amounts to suit your needs and taste. The important thing to remember is to keep the ratios of the ingredients the same so that the cocktail you mix is the same as the recipe intends.

A FEW QUICK POINTERS TO REMEMBER AS YOU MIX YOUR DRINKS:

- Always strive to use fresh juices.

- Measure everything carefully.

- When cutting a citrus twist, do so over the drink to allow some of the oils to drip into the drink.

- Always use plenty of ice.

- Shake or stir the drink long enough to get it as cold as possible.

Agavoni

(by Bastian Heuser, for Mixology Magazine, Berlin, Germany)

- ¾ ounce (22ml) silver tequila
- ¾ ounce (22ml) Campari
- ¾ ounce (22ml) sweet vermouth
- 2 dashes orange bitters

Add to an ice-filled Delmonico glass and stir to chill and mix.

Garnish with a twist of grapefruit.

Bastian recommends using Tapatio Blanco tequila, Carpano Antica vermouth and The Bitter Truth orange bitters.

Alaska

- 2 ounces (60ml) gin
- ¼ ounce (7ml) Chartreuse
- Dash orange bitters

Stir with ice and strain into a cocktail glass.

Garnish with a twist of lemon peel.

Alexander

- 1½ ounce (45ml) brandy
- 1 ounce (30ml) cream
- 1 ounce (30ml) crème de cacao (brown)

Shake with ice and strain into a cocktail glass.

Garnish with a sprinkle of nutmeg.

Algonquin

- 2 ounces (60ml) rye whiskey
- 1 ounce (30ml) dry vermouth
- 1 ounce (30ml) pineapple juice

Shake with ice and strain into a cocktail glass.

Garnish with a cherry.

1950

Alexander

Americano

- 1 ounce (30ml) Campari
- 1 ounce (30ml) sweet vermouth
- Club soda

Pour Campari and sweet vermouth into highball glass filled with ice and stir.

Top with club soda and garnish with an orange wedge or twist of lemon.

Ante

- 1¾ ounce (52ml) calvados or apple brandy
- ¾ ounce (22ml) Dubonnet
- ½ ounce (15ml) Cointreau
- 1 dash Angostura bitters

Stir with ice and strain into a cocktail glass.

Añejo MANhattan

(by Ryan Magarian)

- 2 ounces (60ml) tequila
- ½ ounce (15ml) sweet vermouth
- ¼ ounce (7ml) Licor 43
- 1 dash Angostura bitters
- 1 dash Regan's No. 6 orange bitters

Stir with ice and strain into a cocktail glass.

Ryan recommends using El Tesoro Añejo Tequila for this drink, and when he makes it he garnishes it with mole salami, which is a salami flavored with various spices, chocolate and cinnamon. Wrap the mole salami around a brandy soaked cherry which has been stuck on a pick.

Circa 1900 Angostura bitters booklet

Añejo MANhattan

Aviation

Aviation

- 2 ounces (60ml) gin
- ½ ounce (15ml) maraschino liqueur
- ¼ ounce (7ml) lemon juice

Shake with ice and strain into a cocktail glass.

Garnish with a cherry.

Bacardi Cocktail

- 2 ounces (60ml) light Bacardi rum
- 1 ounce (30ml) lemon or lime juice
- 2 dashes grenadine syrup

Shake with ice and strain into a cocktail glass.

1930s

Bamboo

- 1½ ounce (45ml) dry vermouth
- 1½ ounce (45ml) dry sherry
- 1 dash Angostura bitters
- 1 dash orange bitters

Stir with ice and strain into a cocktail glass.

Garnish with an orange twist.

Beach Blanket

(by Francesco Lafranconi, for the Hard Rock Cafe Steakhouse, Tampa, Florida)

- 1 ounce (30ml) Jägermeister
- 1 ounce (30ml) coffee liqueur
- 1 ounce (30ml) raspberry liqueur
- 1 ounce (30ml) heavy whipping cream

Shake the Jägermeister, coffee liqueur and raspberry liqueurs with ice.

Strain into a cocktail glass.

Float the whipping cream on the top.

Garnish with a pinch of cinnamon-sugar.

Bellini

- 1 ounce (30ml) white peach purée
- 5 ounces (150ml) sparkling wine (Italian Prosecco)

Pour peach purée into a champagne flute and add sparkling wine.

To be authentic, the peach purée should be made from fresh white peaches which have been peeled and then squeezed to release their juices. Or you can use a commercial white peach purée made by a company such as Perfect Purée of Napa Valley.

Bermuda Rum Swizzle

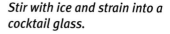

- 2 ounces (60ml) dark rum
- 1 ounce (30ml) lime juice
- 1 ounce (30ml) pineapple juice
- 1 ounce (30ml) orange juice
- ¼ ounce (7ml) falernum

Shake with ice and strain into an ice-filled highball or Collins glass.

Garnish with a slice of orange and a cherry.

To make this as a true swizzle, use a traditional swizzle stick to mix and froth the drink.

Between The Sheets

- 1 ounce (30ml) brandy
- 1 ounce (30ml) light rum
- 1 ounce (30ml) Cointreau
- ½ ounce (15ml) lemon juice

Shake with ice and strain into a cocktail glass.

Garnish with a twist of lemon.

Bijou

- 1 ounce (30ml) gin
- 1 ounce (30ml) green Chartreuse
- 1 ounce (30ml) sweet vermouth
- 1 dash orange bitters

Stir with ice and strain into a cocktail glass.

Garnish with a cherry and a lemon twist.

Bijou

Circa 1930

Bistro Sidecar

*(Created by Kathy Casey,
Kathy Casey Food Studios, Ballard,
Washington)*

- 1½ ounce (45ml) brandy
- ½ ounce (15ml) Tuaca
- ½ ounce (15ml) Frangelico
- ¼ ounce (7ml) of lemon juice
- ¼ ounce (7ml) of simple syrup
- Wedge of tangerine, squeezed

Shake with ice and strain into a sugar-rimmed cocktail glass.

Garnish with a roasted hazelnut.

Black Feather

(Created by Robert Hess, 2000)

- 2 ounces (60ml) brandy
- 1 ounce (30ml) dry vermouth
- ½ ounce (15ml) Cointreau
- 1 dash of bitters

Stir with ice and strain into a cocktail glass.

Garnish with a lemon twist.

I specifically created this drink to be the house cocktail for my home bar which I've nicknamed the Black Feather. In my original recipe I used my own homemade bitters, but, lacking that, Angostura works just fine.

Black Russian

- 2 ounces (60ml) vodka
- 1 ounce (30ml) coffee liqueur

Pour over ice into a rocks glass.

Black Russian

Blackberry Fizz

(by Jonathan Pogash, for Madison and Vine Wine Bar and American Bistro in New York)

- ¾ ounce (22ml) gin
- ¾ ounce (22ml) Lillet Blanc
- 3 fresh blackberries
- ¼ ounce (7ml) lemon juice
- ¼ ounce (7ml) simple syrup
- 3 ounces (90ml) champagne

Muddle the blackberries in the lemon juice and simple syrup.

Add the gin and Lillet and shake with ice, then strain into a flute glass.

Top with champagne and garnish with a fresh blackberry.

Jonathan recommends using Bombay Sapphire for the gin and Moët & Chandon for the champagne.

Blackstar

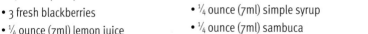

(by Jim Meehan, for PDT in New York)

- 2 ounces (60ml) vodka
- ¾ ounce (22ml) lime juice
- ¾ ounce (22ml) grapefruit juice
- ¼ ounce (7ml) simple syrup
- ¼ ounce (7ml) sambuca
- 1 whole star anise pod (for garnish)

Shake with ice and strain into a cocktail glass.

Garnish by floating the star anise pod in the center.

Jim recommends using Luxardo or Borsci sambuca for this drink.

Blood and Sand

- ¾ ounce (22ml) Scotch whisky
- ¾ ounce (22ml) Cherry Heering
- ¾ ounce (22ml) sweet vermouth
- ¾ ounce (22ml) orange juice

Shake with ice and strain into a cocktail glass.

Bloody Mary

- 1½ ounce (45ml) vodka
- 3 ounces (90ml) tomato juice
- ½ ounce (15ml) lemon juice
- Worcestershire sauce to taste
- Tabasco sauce to taste
- Black pepper to taste
- Celery salt to taste

Roll with ice until properly chilled, and then pour into a tall glass.

Garnish with a celery stalk and a wedge of lemon.

Bloomsbury

(Created by Robert Hess, 2003)

- 2 ounces (60ml) gin
- ½ ounce (15ml) Licor 43
- ½ ounce (15ml) Lillet Blanc
- 2 dashes Peychaud's bitters

Stir with ice and strain into a cocktail glass.

Garnish with lemon twist.

Bobbo's Bride

(Created by Laurel Semmes, 1999)

- 1 ounce (30ml) gin
- 1 ounce (30ml) vodka
- ½ ounce (15ml) peach liqueur
- ¼ ounce (7ml) Campari

Stir with ice and strain into a cocktail glass.

Garnish with a slice of fresh peach

Bloody Mary

1928

Bordeaux Cocktail

(Created by Tito Class for Mona's Bistro & Lounge, Seattle)

- 2¼ ounces (67ml) citrus vodka
- ¾ ounce (22ml) Lillet Blanc

Stir with ice and strain into a cocktail glass.

Garnish with a lemon twist.

Bourbon Crusta

(By Gary & Mardee Regan, The Book of Bourbon)

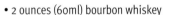

- 2 ounces (60ml) bourbon whiskey
- ½ ounce (15ml) triple sec
- ½ ounce (15ml) maraschino liqueur
- ½ ounce (15ml) lemon juice
- 2 dashes orange bitters

Shake with ice and strain into a sugar rimmed cocktail glass.

Garnish with an orange peel.

Bobby Burns

- 1½ ounce (45ml) blended scotch whisky
- 1½ ounce (45ml) sweet vermouth
- ¼ ounce (7ml) Bénédictine

Stir with ice and strain into a cocktail glass.

Garnish with a lemon twist.

Bourbon Crusta

Brandy Cobbler

- Large chunk of pineapple
- Orange wedge
- Lemon wedge
- ¾ ounce (22ml) raspberry syrup or raspberry liqueur
- 1 ounce (30ml) water
- 2 ounces (60ml) brandy

Muddle the pineapple, orange, and lemon with the raspberry syrup and water in a mixing glass.

Add the brandy and shake with ice.

Strain into a large wine goblet filled with crushed ice.

Garnish with lemon, orange, pineapple and fresh raspberries.

Brandy Crusta

- 1½ ounce (45ml) brandy
- ¼ ounce (7ml) maraschino liqueur
- ¼ ounce (7ml) Cointreau
- ¼ ounce (7ml) lemon juice

Shake with ice and strain into a small sugar rimmed wine glass.

Garnish with a long wide spiral of lemon peel.

Brandy Shrub

(makes 12 drinks)

- 2 cups (500ml) brandy
- 1 whole lemon
- 1 cup (225g) sugar
- 1 cup (250ml) water
- ⅔ cup (160ml) sherry

Peel the rind off of the lemon, and then juice it.

Place the rind, juice, and brandy in a jar, then seal and store in a cool dark place for three days, and then strain.

Then make simple syrup by simmering the water, and stirring in the sugar until dissolved. Allow this to cool, then add it to the brandy/lemon mixture, and then add the sherry. Bottle and store in the refrigerator.

To make a drink, place 2 ounces (60ml) of the mixture into an ice-filled highball glass, then top with club soda.

Brandy Smash

- 2 ounces (60ml) brandy
- ½ ounce (15ml) simple syrup
- 3 sprigs mint

Add simple syrup and mint to a rocks glass, and muddle lightly to express mint flavors into the syrup.

Fill with crushed ice and then add the brandy.

Stir to chill.

Garnish with a mint sprig.

Serve with straws.

You can make this with any spirit, i.e., a gin smash, rum smash, etc.

Bridal

- 2 ounces (60ml) gin
- 1 ounce (30ml) sweet vermouth
- ¼ ounce (7ml) maraschino liqueur
- Dash orange bitters

Stir with ice and strain into a cocktail glass.

Garnish with a cherry.

Bronx

- 1½ ounce (45ml) gin
- ¾ ounce (22ml) orange juice
- ¼ ounce (7ml) sweet vermouth
- ¼ ounce (7ml) dry vermouth

Shake with ice and strain into a cocktail glass.

1930s

Brooklyn

- 2¼ ounces (67ml) rye or bourbon whiskey
- ¾ ounce (22ml) sweet vermouth
- 1 dash Amer Picon
- 1 dash maraschino liqueur

Stir with ice and strain into a cocktail glass.

Buck's Fizz

- 2 ounces (60ml) orange juice
- 1 dash cherry brandy
- ¼ ounce (7ml) gin
- 4 ounces (120ml) sparkling wine

Slowly pour the ingredients in the order listed into a champagne flute or wine glass. Garnish with an orange wedge.

Bull Shot

- 1½ ounce (45ml) vodka
- 3 ounces (90ml) beef bouillon
- ¼ ounce (7ml) lemon juice
- Worcestershire sauce to taste
- Tabasco sauce to taste
- Black pepper to taste
- Celery salt to taste

Shake with ice and strain into an ice-filled highball glass.

1937

Garnish with some cracked black pepper and a wedge of lime.

This is essentially a Bloody Mary using beef bouillon instead of tomato juice. You may have to adjust your seasoning if you're using a pre-seasoned bouillon.

Cabaret

- 1½ ounce (45ml) gin
- 1 ounce (30ml) dry vermouth
- ¼ ounce (7ml) Bénédictine
- 2 dashes Angostura bitters

Stir with ice and strain into a cocktail glass.

Garnish with a cherry.

Cable Car

(by Tony Abou-Ganim, for the Starlight Room in San Francisco, 1993)

- 1½ ounce (45ml) spiced rum
- ¾ ounce (22ml) orange curaçao
- 1 ounce (30ml) lemon juice
- ½ ounce (15ml) simple syrup

Shake with ice and then strain into a cocktail glass which has been rimmed with a cinnamon sugar mixture.

Garnish with an orange twist.

Tony recommends making this drink with Captain Morgan's Spiced Rum and Marie Brizard orange curaçao.

Caipirinha

Caesar

- 1 ounce (30ml) vodka
- 4 ounces (120ml) tomato-clam juice (a.k.a. Clamato juice)
- Pinch of salt and pepper
- Dash Worcestershire sauce
- 2 to 3 dashes horseradish
- Celery salt
- Celery stalk

Shake ingredients with ice.

Coat rim of a highball or Delmonico glass with celery salt, and then fill with ice.

Strain mixture into glass.

Garnish with a celery stalk and a lemon wedge.

1938

Caipirinha

- 2 ounces (60ml) cachaça (Brazilian white rum)
- 1 teaspoon (5ml) sugar
- 1 lime

Wash the lime, and cut it into quarters.

Put limes and sugar into a tumbler, and muddle hard.

Add the cachaça and stir.

Fill with ice, and stir again.

I like to use granulated sugar instead of simple syrup for this drink to allow the sugar to help grind out some of the flavorful oils from the lime's skin.

Calvados Cocktail

- 1½ ounce (45ml) calvados (apple brandy)
- 1½ ounce (45ml) orange juice
- ¾ ounce (22ml) Cointreau
- ¾ ounce (22ml) orange bitters

Shake with ice and then strain into a cocktail glass.

Canton

- 2 ounces (60ml) Jamaican rum
- ½ ounce (15ml) maraschino liqueur
- ½ ounce (15ml) orange curaçao
- 1 dash grenadine

Stir with ice and then strain into a cocktail glass.

Garnish with a cherry and orange twist.

Caprice

- 1½ ounce (45ml) gin
- ½ ounce (15ml) dry vermouth
- ½ ounce (15ml) Bénédictine
- 1 dash orange bitters

Stir with ice and then strain into a cocktail glass.

Captain's Blood

- 2 ounces (60ml) dark rum
- ½ ounce (15ml) lime juice
- ½ ounce (15ml) simple syrup
- 2 dashes Angostura bitters

Shake with ice and then strain into a cocktail glass.

Garnish with a spiral of lemon peel.

Casino

- 2 ounces (60ml) gin
- ⅛ ounce (4ml) lemon juice
- ⅛ ounce (4ml) maraschino liqueur
- 2 dashes orange bitters

Shake with ice and then strain into a cocktail glass.

Garnish with a cherry.

Champagne Antoine

(Created by Robert Hess, for Antoine's Restaurant, New Orleans)

- 1 ounce (30ml) gin
- 1 ounce (30ml) dry vermouth
- ⅛ ounce (4ml) Pernod
- 4 ounces (120ml) dry champagne

Shake the gin, vermouth, and Pernod with ice and then strain into a champagne flute.

Top with champagne and garnish with a lemon twist.

Champagne Cocktail

- 6 ounces (180ml) chilled champagne
- 1 sugar cube (1 teaspoon/5ml)
- Angostura bitters

Soak sugar cube with Angostura bitters and then drop the sugar cube into a flute glass filled with champagne.

Garnish with a lemon twist.

Champagne Cocktail

Moët ad, 1950s

Champagne Flamingo

- ¾ ounce (22ml) vodka
- ¾ ounce (22ml) Campari
- 5 ounces (150ml) chilled champagne

Shake vodka and Campari with ice and then strain into a flute glass.

Top with champagne and then garnish with an orange twist.

Champs Elysées

- 1 ounce (30ml) brandy (cognac)
- ¼ ounce (7ml) green Chartreuse
- 1 ounce (30ml) lemon juice
- 1 dash Angostura bitters

Shake with ice and strain into a cocktail glass.

Garnish with a lemon twist.

Chaplin

- ¾ ounce (22ml) bourbon whiskey
- ¾ ounce (22ml) dry sherry
- ¾ ounce (22ml) Ramazzotti
- ⅛ ounce (4ml) Cointreau
- 2 dashes orange bitters

Stir with ice and then strain into a cocktail glass.

Garnish with a lemon twist.

Ramazzotti is an Italian bitter digestif wine with a noted orange flavor. It can be relatively hard to find.

Chas

(By Murray Stenson, for the Zig Zag Café, Seattle)

- 2¼ ounces (67ml) bourbon whiskey
- ¼ ounce (7ml) amaretto
- ¼ ounce (7ml) Bénédictine
- ¼ ounce (7ml) Cointreau
- ¼ ounce (7ml) orange curaçao

Stir with ice and strain into a cocktail glass.

Garnish with an orange twist.

Chrysanthemum Cocktail

- 2 ounces (60ml) dry vermouth
- 1 ounce (30ml) Bénédictine
- 3 dashes absinthe or pastis

Stir with ice and strain into a cocktail glass.

Garnish with a twist of orange

Cloister

- 1½ ounce (45ml) gin
- ½ ounce (15ml) yellow Chartreuse
- ½ ounce (15ml) grapefruit juice
- ¼ ounce (7ml) lemon juice
- ¼ ounce (7ml) simple syrup

Shake with ice and strain into a cocktail glass.

Garnish with a grapefruit twist.

Clover Club

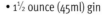

- 1½ ounce (45ml) gin
- ¼ ounce (7ml) grenadine
- ¾ ounce (22ml) lemon juice
- 1 egg white

First shake this without any ice to help foam the egg, then add ice to the shaker and shake to chill.

Strain into a fancy cocktail or wine glass.

Coffee Cocktail

- 1½ ounce (45ml) port
- 1½ ounce (45ml) brandy
- 1 teaspoon (5ml) simple syrup
- 1 whole egg

Shake hard with ice and strain into a wine glass.

Garnish with grated nutmeg.

Clover Club

Coffee Nudge

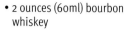

- ½ ounce (15ml) brandy
- ½ ounce (15ml) coffee liqueur
- ½ ounce (15ml) dark crème de cacao
- 5 ounces (150ml) coffee

Whip cream for garnish.

In a pre-warmed coffee mug, add the brandy, coffee liqueur and crème de cacao.

Pour in the coffee (decaf can be used if desired) and top with a dollop of whip cream.

Serve with cocktail straws.

Commodore

- 2 ounces (60ml) bourbon whiskey
- ¾ ounce (22ml) white crème de cacao
- ½ ounce (15ml) lemon juice
- 1 dash grenadine

Shake with ice and strain into champagne flute.

Companero

(by Sean Muldoon, for the Merchant Hotel, Belfast, Northern Ireland)

- 1 ounce (30ml) rum
- ½ ounce (15ml) white crème de cacao
- ½ ounce (15ml) lime juice
- 3 torn basil leaves
- ¼ ounce (7ml) sugar syrup

Shake with ice and double-strain into a cocktail glass.

Garnish with a lime wedge.

Sean recommends using an aged Cuban rum.

OLD CROW
Collection of
GREAT
BOURBON DRINK
RECIPES

1950s

Coffee Cocktail

Corleone

(by Ryan Magarian)

- 5 white grapes
- 1½ ounce (45ml) gin
- ½ ounce (15ml) grappa
- ½ ounce (15ml) lemon juice
- ¾ ounce (22ml) simple syrup
- 1 dash orange bitters

Muddle the grapes in a mixing glass, then add everything else and shake with ice.

Strain into a cocktail glass.

Garnish with a single white grape sliced midway and resting on the glass rim.

Corleone

Corpse Reviver #1

- 2 ounces (60ml) brandy (cognac)
- 1 ounce (30ml) sweet vermouth
- 1 ounce (30ml) applejack

Stir with ice and strain into a cocktail glass.

Corpse Reviver #2

- ¾ ounce (22ml) gin
- ¾ ounce (22ml) lemon juice
- ¾ ounce (22ml) Cointreau
- ¾ ounce (22ml) Lillet Blanc
- Dash absinthe or pastis

Shake with ice and strain into a cocktail glass.

Corpse Reviver #3

- 1 ounce (30ml) brandy (cognac)
- 1 ounce (30ml) Campari
- 1 ounce (30ml) triple sec
- ½ ounce (15ml) lemon juice

Shake with ice and strain into a cocktail glass.

Cosmopolitan

- ½ ounce (45ml) citrus vodka
- ½ ounce (15ml) Cointreau
- 1 ounce (30ml) cranberry juice
- ¾ ounce (22ml) lime juice

Shake with ice and strain into a cocktail glass.

Garnish with lime wedge.

Country Gentleman

- 1½ ounce (45ml) apple brandy
- ¾ ounce (22ml) orange curaçao
- ¼ ounce (7ml) lemon juice
- 1 teaspoon (5ml) simple syrup

Shake with ice and strain into cocktail glass.

Garnish with a lemon twist.

Crux

- ¾ ounce (22ml) brandy
- ¾ ounce (22ml) Dubonnet
- ¾ ounce (22ml) Cointreau
- ¾ ounce (22ml) lemon juice

Stir with ice and strain into a cocktail glass.

Cuba Libre

Cuba Libre

- 2 ounces (60ml) rum
- 4 ounces (120ml) cola
- Lime wedge

Pour into an ice-filled tumbler.

Add a generous squeeze of lime, and then add the rind as a garnish.

Almost a Rum & Coke. However, when properly made, a Cuba Libre will include a squeeze of lime while a Rum & Coke is just garnished with a lime wedge.

Daiquiri

- 2 ounces (60ml) light rum
- ¾ ounce (22ml) simple syrup
- ½ ounce (15ml) lime juice

Shake with ice and strain into a cocktail glass.

Garnish with a lime slice.

Dark 'n Stormy

- 2 ounces (60ml) Gosling's Black Seal rum
- 4 ounces (120ml) ginger beer

Pour into an ice-filled highball glass.

Garnish with a lime wedge.

Dark 'n Stormy

Death in the Afternoon

- 1 ounce (30ml) absinthe or pastis
- 5 ounces (150ml) chilled sparkling wine

Pour absinthe or pastis into a champagne flute and then top with sparkling wine.

Delilah

- 1½ ounce (45ml) gin
- ¾ ounce (22ml) Cointreau
- ¾ ounce (22ml) lemon juice

Shake with ice and strain into a cocktail glass.

Delmonico

- 1 ounce (30ml) gin
- ½ ounce (15ml) brandy
- ½ ounce (15ml) dry vermouth
- ½ ounce (15ml) sweet vermouth
- 1 dash orange bitters

Stir with ice and strain into a cocktail glass.

Garnish with a lemon twist.

Derby

- 2 ounces (60ml) bourbon whiskey
- ¼ ounce (7ml) Bénédictine
- 1 dash Angostura bitters

Stir with ice and strain into a cocktail glass.

Garnish with a lemon peel

Deshler

- 1½ ounce (45ml) rye whiskey
- 1 ounce (30ml) Dubonnet rouge
- ¼ ounce (7ml) Cointreau
- 2 dashes Peychaud's bitters
- 1 orange twist (in mixing glass)
- 1 lemon twist (in mixing glass)

Stir with ice and strain into a cocktail glass.

Garnish with an orange peel.

Diablo

- 1½ ounce (45ml) tequila
- ¾ ounce (22ml) crème de cassis
- ½ ounce (15ml) lime juice
- Ginger ale

Shake tequila, cassis, and lime juice with ice and strain into a Collins glass.

Top with ginger ale and garnish with a lime wheel.

Diabolo

- 2 ounces (60ml) rum
- ½ ounce (15ml) Cointreau
- ½ ounce (15ml) dry vermouth
- 2 dashes Angostura bitters

Stir with ice and strain into a cocktail glass.

Garnish with a twist of orange peel.

East India House

- 1¾ ounce (52ml) brandy
- ¼ ounce (7ml) rum
- ¼ ounce (7ml) pineapple juice
- ¼ ounce (7ml) orange curaçao
- 1 dash orange bitters

Shake with ice.

Strain into a cocktail glass.

Garnish with a lemon twist and cherry.

Eastern Sour

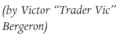

(by Victor "Trader Vic" Bergeron)

- 2 ounces (60ml) bourbon whiskey
- 1½ ounce (45ml) orange juice
- 1 ounce (30ml) lime juice
- ¼ ounce (7ml) orgeat (almond syrup)
- ¼ ounce (7ml) simple syrup

Shake with ice and strain into an ice-filled rocks glass.

Garnish with spent shell of lime.

Eggnog

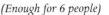

(Enough for 6 people)

- 6 eggs
- 1 cup (200g) sugar
- ½ teaspoon (2.5ml) salt
- 1 cup (250ml) golden rum
- 1 pint (475ml) cream
- 1 pint (475ml) milk
- Nutmeg

In a large bowl, beat eggs until light and foamy.

Add sugar and salt, beating until thick and lemon colored.

Stir in rum, cream, and milk.

Eggnog

Chill at least three hours.

Serve with a sprinkle of nutmeg.

Elderthorn

(by Robert Hess, 2007)

- 1 ounce (30ml) cognac or brandy
- ½ ounce (15ml) St. Germain Elderflower liqueur
- ½ ounce (15ml) Cynar

Stir with ice and strain into a cocktail glass.

El Presidente

- 1½ ounce (45ml) white rum
- ½ ounce (15ml) dry vermouth
- ½ ounce (15ml) orange curaçao
- Dash of grenadine

Stir with ice and strain into a cocktail glass.

Garnish with an orange twist.

Fallen Leaves

(By Charles Schumann, 1982)

- ¾ ounce (22ml) calvados (apple brandy)
- ¾ ounce (22ml) sweet vermouth
- ¼ ounce (7ml) dry vermouth
- Dash brandy
- Squeeze lemon peel

Stir with ice and strain into a cocktail glass.

Squeeze lemon twist into drink, and use as garnish.

Fancy-Free Cocktail

- 2 ounces (60ml) bourbon whiskey
- ½ ounce (15ml) maraschino liqueur
- 1 dash Angostura bitters
- 1 dash orange bitters

Stir with ice and strain into a cocktail glass.

Fancy-Free

Fin de Siècle

- 1½ ounce (45ml) gin
- ¾ ounce (22ml) sweet vermouth
- ¼ ounce (7ml) Amer Picon
- 1 dash orange bitters

Stir with ice and strain into a cocktail glass.

Fish House Punch

(Enough for 32 people)

- 1½ cups (300g) superfine sugar
- 2 quarts (2L) water
- 1 quart (1L) lemon juice
- 2 quarts (2L) dark rum
- 1 quart (1L) brandy (cognac)
- 4 ounces (120ml) peach brandy

In a large punch bowl, combine sugar and about half of the water.

Stir until fully dissolved.

Then add the lemon juice and spirits, then slip in as large of a block of ice as you can. Allow to sit for at least 30 minutes before serving.

Use the reserved water to adjust for balance if necessary.

1937

Floridita

- 1½ ounce (45ml) rum
- ½ ounce (15ml) lime juice
- ½ ounce (15ml) sweet vermouth
- ⅛ ounce (4ml) white crème de cacao
- ⅛ ounce (4ml) grenadine

Shake with ice and strain into a cocktail glass.

Garnish with a lime twist.

Floridita

Fog Cutter

(by Victor "Trader Vic" Bergeron, 1950)

- 2 ounces (60ml) lemon juice
- 1 ounce (30ml) orange juice
- ½ ounce (15ml) orgeat (almond syrup)
- 2 ounces (60ml) white rum
- 1 ounce (30ml) brandy
- ½ ounce (15ml) gin
- ½ ounce (15ml) sweet sherry

Shake everything—except sherry —with ice and then pour into tall ice-filled Tiki mug or Collins glass.

Float the sherry over the top.

Frappéed Café Royal

- 1½ ounces (45ml) cognac
- 2 ounces (60ml) espresso

Shake with ice and then strain into a Delmonico glass filled with finely crushed/shaved ice.

Stir with a stirring rod or swizzle stick until well chilled and some ice begins to frost on the outside of the glass.

Top with a little more shaved ice.

Serve with straws.

French 75

- 1 ounce (30ml) gin
- ¼ ounce (7ml) lemon juice
- ⅛ ounce (4ml) simple syrup
- 5 ounces (150ml) champagne

Shake gin, lemon juice and syrup with ice and strain into a flute glass.

Top with champagne.

French Quarter

(By Robert Hess, 2004)

- 2½ ounces (75ml) brandy
- ¾ ounce (22ml) Lillet Blanc

Stir with ice and strain into a cocktail glass.

Garnish with a thin quarter wheel of lemon.

Frostbite

- 1 ounce (30ml) tequila
- ¾ ounce (22ml) white crème de cacao
- ¾ ounce (22ml) cream

Shake hard with ice to froth the cream a little and strain into a cocktail glass.

Garnish with a sprinkle of nutmeg.

Gibson

- 2½ ounces (75ml) gin
- ½ ounce (15ml) dry vermouth

Stir with ice and strain into a cocktail glass.

Garnish with a cocktail onion.

Gibson

Gimlet

- 2¼ ounces (67ml) gin
- ¾ ounce (22ml) Rose's lime juice

Stir with ice and strain into a cocktail glass.

Gin Buck

- 2 ounces (60ml) gin
- ½ ounce (15ml) lime or lemon juice
- 4 ounces (120ml) ginger ale

Add gin and juice to an ice-filled highball glass, then top with ginger ale.

Stir briefly.

You can make this drink with any base spirit, thus creating a rum buck, tequila buck, etc.

Gin Daisy

- 2½ ounces (75ml) gin
- 1 ounce (30ml) lemon or lime juice
- ½ ounce (15ml) grenadine

Shake with ice and strain into an ice-filled highball glass.

Garnish with a lemon twist.

You can make this drink with any base spirit, thus creating a brandy daisy, rum daisy, etc.

Gin Fix

- 2½ ounces (75ml) gin
- 1 ounce (30ml) lemon or lime juice
- ½ ounce (15ml) pineapple syrup

Shake with ice and strain into an ice-filled Delmonico glass.

Garnish with a lemon twist.

If you can't fine pineapple syrup, you can use 1/4 ounce (7ml) pineapple juice and 1/4 ounce (7ml) simple syrup.

You can make this drink with any base spirit, thus creating an applejack fix, whiskey fix, etc.

Gin Fizz

- 2 ounces (60ml) gin
- 1 ounce (30ml) lemon juice
- ½ ounce (15ml) simple syrup
- 5 ounces (150ml) club soda

Shake all but the club soda with ice and then strain into an ice-filled Delmonico/fizz glass.

Top with club soda and stir briefly to fizz it up.

Gin Flip

- 2 ounces (60ml) gin
- ½ ounce (15ml) simple syrup
- 1 whole egg

Shake hard with ice and strain into a Delmonico glass or wine glass.

Garnish with nutmeg.

Gin Rickey

- 2 ounces (60ml) gin
- ¾ ounce (22ml) lime juice
- ½ ounce (15ml) simple syrup
- 2 ounces (60ml) club soda

Stir all but the club soda in a Collins glass with a couple ice cubes, then top with club soda. Garnish with a lime wedge.

Gin Sling

- 2 ounces (60ml) gin
- ½ ounce (15ml) chilled water
- ½ ounce (15ml) simple syrup

Combine in a rocks glass with a single ice cube.

Stir briefly to combine and serve without straws.

You can make this with any spirit. If desired, you can add a teaspoon of lemon juice.

Gin Tonic Cocktail

(by Sean Muldoon, for the Merchant Hotel, Belfast, Northern Ireland)

- ¾ ounce (22ml) dry gin
- ¾ ounce (22ml) Lillet Blanc
- ¾ ounce (22ml) lime juice
- ½ ounce (15ml) simple syrup
- 2 small sprigs fresh cilantro (coriander leaves)
- 1 dash Peychaud's bitters

Shake with ice and double-strain into a cocktail glass.

Garnish with a lime wedge.

Goat's Delight

- 1¾ ounce (52ml) kirschwasser
- 1¾ ounce (52ml) brandy
- ¼ ounce (7ml) orgeat (almond syrup)
- ¼ ounce (7ml) cream
- Dash of absinthe or pastis

Shake with ice and strain into a cocktail glass.

Golden Dawn

- ¾ ounce (22ml) gin
- ¾ ounce (22ml) calvados or apple brandy
- ¾ ounce (22ml) apricot brandy
- ¾ ounce (22ml) orange juice

Shake with ice and strain into a cocktail glass.

Golden Dream

- ¾ ounce (22ml) Galliano
- ½ ounce (15ml) Cointreau
- ½ ounce (15ml) orange juice
- 1 tablespoon (15ml) cream

Shake with ice and strain into a cocktail glass.

Gotham

(by Robert Hess, 2002)

- ½ teaspoon (2.5ml) absinthe or pastis
- 3 dashes peach bitters
- 2 ounces (60ml) brandy

Coat a chilled small rocks glass with absinthe or pastis, then add the peach bitters and brandy.

Garnish with a lemon twist.

Galliano

The Govenor's

(by Gwydion Stone)

- 1½ ounce (45ml) gin
- 1½ ounce (45ml) Pimm's No. 1
- ½ ounce (15ml) lime juice
- ½ ounce (15ml) simple syrup
- ½ ounce (15ml) absinthe

Shake with ice and strain into a cocktail glass.

Grasshopper

- 1 ounce (30ml) green crème de menthe
- 1 ounce (30ml) white crème de cacao
- 2 ounces (60ml) heavy cream

Shake well with ice and strain into a cocktail glass.

Grasshopper

Guinness Punch

- 8 ounces (240ml) Guinness stout
- 5 ounces (150ml) sweetened condensed milk
- 1 raw egg
- Sprinkle of cinnamon
- Sprinkle of nutmeg

Mix all ingredients in a blender or with a whisk.

Pour into a tall glass.

Garnish with an additional sprinkle of cinnamon and nutmeg.

Guadalajara

(by Robert Hess, 2001)

- 2 ounces (60ml) tequila
- 1 ounce (30ml) dry vermouth
- ½ ounce (15ml) Bénédictine

Stir with ice and strain into a cocktail glass.

Garnish with lemon twist.

Harrington

(by Paul Harrington)

- 1½ ounce (45ml) vodka
- ¼ ounce (7ml) Cointreau
- ⅛ ounce (4ml) green Chartreuse

Stir with ice and strain into a cocktail glass.

Twist an orange zest over the drink and then float zest in drink.

1998

Promotional drink pamphlet

Harvard

- 1½ ounce (45ml) brandy
- ¾ ounce (22ml) sweet vermouth
- ¼ ounce (7ml) grenadine
- ½ ounce (15ml) lemon juice

Dash of Angostura bitters

Shake with ice and strain into a cocktail glass.

Hemingway Daiquiri

- 1½ ounce (45ml) white rum
- ¼ ounce (7ml) maraschino liqueur
- ½ ounce (15ml) grapefruit juice
- ¾ ounce (22ml) simple syrup
- ¾ ounce (22ml) lime juice

Shake with ice and strain into a chilled cocktail glass.

Highland Cocktail

- 1½ ounce (45ml) Scotch whisky
- 1½ ounce (45ml) sweet vermouth
- 1 dash orange bitters

Stir with ice and strain into a cocktail glass.

Hoskins

(by Chuck Taggart, 2003)

- 2 ounces (60ml) Plymouth gin
- ¾ ounce (22ml) Torani Amer
- ½ ounce (15ml) maraschino liqueur
- ¼ ounce (7ml) Cointreau
- 1 dash orange bitters

Stir with ice and strain into a cocktail glass.

Flame an orange peel over the drink and garnish with the peel.

Hot Buttered Rum

Batter mix:
- 1 pound (.45kg) brown sugar
- ¼ pound (.11kg) butter
- Pinch of salt
- ¼ teaspoon (1ml) nutmeg
- ¼ teaspoon (1ml) cloves
- ½ teaspoon (2.5ml) cinnamon

Combine all ingredients and stir together until well blended and creamy.

In a pre-heated coffee mug, drop in 1 heaping teaspoon (5+ml) of the above batter.

Add 2 ounces (60ml) of rum.

Top with hot water.

Stir well.

Garnish with grated nutmeg or dash of cinnamon.

Hot Toddy

- 1½ ounce (45ml) brandy
- ¼ ounce (7ml) lemon juice
- 1 sugar cube (1 teaspoon/5ml), rubbed against the rind of a lemon to infuse it with oils
- 4 ounces (120ml) hot water

Pour into a pre-warmed coffee mug

Stir with a cinnamon stick to dissolve the sugar.

Garnish with a half-slice of lemon.

Hot Buttered Rum

Hot Toddy

Income Tax

- 1¼ ounce (37ml) gin
- ¾ ounce (22ml) orange juice
- ¼ ounce (7ml) dry vermouth
- ¼ ounce (7ml) sweet vermouth
- 1 dash Angostura bitters

Shake with ice and strain into a cocktail glass.

Irish Coffee

The Interesting Cocktail

(by Gary Regan)

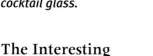

- 2 ounces (60ml) silver tequila
- ¾ ounce (22ml) Aperol
- ¼ ounce (7ml) dark crème de cacao
- ¼ ounce (7ml) lemon juice
- 4 grapefruit twists

Add everything to an ice-filled mixing glass.

Twist three of the grapefruit peels over the glass, and drop them in.

Shake and then strain into a flute glass.

Garnish with the remaining grapefruit twist.

Irish Coffee

- 1 teaspoon (5ml) sugar
- 4 ounces (120ml) hot coffee
- 2 ounces (60ml) Irish whiskey
- Dapple of heavy cream

Pre-heat coffee glass with hot water, then empty.

In a pre-heated glass coffee mug or Irish Coffee glass, add the sugar and coffee.

Stir to dissolve.

Then add the whiskey, and add a float of lightly whipped cream on top.

Part of the trick to this drink is whipping the cream until it is just solid enough not to sink through the coffee, but not stiff either. Never use the whipping cream in a pressurized can.

Jack Rose

- 2½ ounces (75ml) applejack
- ¾ ounce (22ml) lemon juice
- ½ ounce (15ml) grenadine

Shake with ice and strain into a cocktail glass.

Garnish with a lemon twist.

This is a lovely and subtle sour-style cocktail. The grenadine you use will make all the difference here. Best to find one made with real pomegranate juice.

Japanese

- 2 ounces (60ml) brandy
- ½ ounce (15ml) orgeat (almond syrup)
- 2 dashes Angostura bitters

Stir with ice and strain into a cocktail glass.

Garnish with a lemon twist.

1862, by Jerry Thomas

Jasmine

(by Paul Harrington)

- 1½ ounce (45ml) gin
- ¼ ounce (7ml) Cointreau
- ¼ ounce (7ml) Campari
- ¾ ounce (22ml) lemon juice

Shake with ice an strain into a cocktail glass.

Garnish with a lemon twist.

This is Paul Harrington's original recipe. I've tinkered with it a bit to accentuate the flavors. My variation is:

- 1½ ounces (45ml) gin
- 1 ounce (30ml) Cointreau
- ¾ ounce (22ml) Campari
- ½ ounce (15 ml) lemon juice.

I was originally only going to list my version here, but decided to respect Paul's original recipe by listing it first, then providing my interpretation. This illustrates how recipes can be different from one bartender to another.

Joli Rajah

(by Gwydion Stone)

- 2½ ounces (75ml) rum
- ½ ounce (15ml) lemon juice
- ½ ounce (15ml) grenadine
- ½ ounce (15ml) absinthe

Shake with ice and strain into a cocktail glass.

Journalist

- 1½ ounce (45ml) gin
- ¼ ounce (7ml) dry vermouth
- ¼ ounce (7ml) sweet vermouth
- 2 dashes triple sec
- 2 dashes lemon juice
- 1 dash Angostura bitters

Shake with ice and strain into a cocktail glass.

1963

Jupiter

- 2 ounces (60ml) gin
- 1 ounce (30ml) dry vermouth
- 1 teaspoon (5ml) orange juice
- 1 teaspoon (5ml) Parfait Amour (orange liqueur)

Shake with ice, and strain into a cocktail glass.

Be extremely careful measuring the Parfait Amour. Too much will ruin the drink. Parfait Amour may be hard to find; Marie Brizard is the most common brand.

Kamikaze

- 1½ ounce (45ml) vodka
- 1 ounce (30ml) triple sec
- 1 ounce (30ml) lime juice

Shake with ice and strain into a cocktail glass.

Garnish with a lime twist.

Kir Royale

Kir

- 5 ounces (150ml) dry white wine (Chardonnay)
- ¼ ounce (7ml) crème de cassis

Pour wine into a wine glass and then add the crème de cassis.

Kir Royale

- 5 ounces (150ml) champagne
- ¼ ounce (7ml) crème de cassis

Fill flute with champagne and add the crème de cassis.

Garnish with a lemon twist.

1960s

Kangaroo

- 1½ ounce (45ml) vodka
- ½ ounce (15ml) dry vermouth

Stir with ice and strain into a cocktail glass.

Garnish with a lemon twist.

La Louisiane

- ¾ ounce (22ml) rye whiskey
- ¾ ounce (22ml) sweet vermouth
- ¾ ounce (22ml) Bénédictine
- 3 dashes pastis
- 3 dashes Peychaud's bitters

Stir with ice and strain into a cocktail glass.

Garnish with a cherry.

Last Word

- ½ ounce (15ml) gin
- ½ ounce (15ml) maraschino liqueur
- ½ ounce (15ml) green Chartreuse
- ½ ounce (15ml) lime juice

Shake with ice and strain into a cocktail glass.

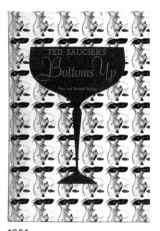

1951

Leap Year

- 2 ounces (60ml) gin
- ½ ounce (15ml) sweet vermouth
- ½ ounce (15ml) Grand Marnier

Dash of lemon juice

Shake with ice and strain into a cocktail glass.

Lemon Drop

- 1½ ounce (45ml) citrus vodka
- ¾ ounce (22ml) lemon juice
- 1 teaspoon (5ml) sugar

Shake with ice and strain into a sugar-rimmed cocktail glass.

Garnish with a lemon wheel.

Liberal

- 1½ ounce (45ml) rye whiskey
- ½ ounce (15ml) sweet vermouth
- ¼ ounce (7ml) Amer Picon
- 1 dash orange bitters

Stir with ice and strain into a cocktail glass.

Garnish with an orange twist.

Lucien Gaudin

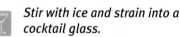

- 1 ounce (30ml) gin
- ½ ounce (15ml) Cointreau
- ½ ounce (15ml) Campari
- ½ ounce (15ml) dry vermouth

Stir with ice and strain into a cocktail glass.

Garnish with a lemon twist.

Mahogany

(by Robert Hess, 2003)

- 1½ ounce (45ml) dry vermouth
- ¾ ounce (22ml) Jägermeister
- ¾ ounce (22ml) Bénédictine

Stir with ice and strain into a cocktail glass.

Extra Credit: Before adding the drink to the glass, use an atomizer to spray the glass with a mild cinnamon tincture. To make your cinnamon tincture, soak four sticks of cinnamon in 1 cup (250ml) of vodka for about two weeks.

I created this drink after being challenged by a friend to come up with a classically styled cocktail which used Jägermeister. The process taught me a new appreciation for this German digestif.

Postcard, 1907

Mai Tai

(By Victor "Trader Vic" Bergeron, 1944)

- 1 ounce (30ml) light rum
- 1 ounce (30ml) gold rum
- ½ ounce (15ml) orange curaçao
- ½ ounce (15ml) orgeat (almond syrup)
- ½ ounce (15ml) lime juice
- ½ ounce (15ml) dark rum (optional)

Shake all but the dark rum with ice.

Strain into an ice-filled rocks glass.

Top with the dark rum if you wish, then garnish with a maraschino cherry.

This recipe has often been personalized to the point of having little in common with the original. The above version will let you see how this drink was originally intended to be made.

Trader Vic's cocktail menu

Malmo Aviation

(by Sean Muldoon, for the Merchant Hotel, Belfast Northern Ireland)

- 1⅓ ounce (40ml) dry gin
- ⅓ ounce (10ml) Luxardo maraschino liqueur
- ¾ ounce (22ml) lime juice
- ⅓ ounce (10ml) sugar syrup
- 10 mint leaves

Shake with ice and double-strain into a cocktail glass.

Garnish with a cherry.

Margarita

Manhattan

- 2½ ounces (75ml) American rye or bourbon whiskey
- ¾ ounce (22ml) sweet vermouth
- Dash Angostura bitters

Stir with ice and strain into a cocktail glass.

Garnish with a cherry.

This is a veritable classic, which never goes out of style. Make sure you stir instead of shake, otherwise you'll end up with an unappetizing foam on top.

Margarita

- 1½ ounce (45ml) tequila
- 1 ounce (30ml) Cointreau
- ½ ounce (15ml) lime juice

Shake with ice and strain into an ice-filled Old Fashioned glass or a salt-rimmed margarita glass.

Consistently ranked as the most popular cocktail in America, the Margarita is definitely a crowd pleaser. To make this drink properly, you should never use a sour mix, nor should the drink ever see the inside of a blender.

Martinez

- 1 ounce (30ml) gin
- 2 ounces (60ml) sweet vermouth
- 1 dash bitters
- 2 dashes maraschino

Stir with ice and strain into a cocktail glass.

Garnish with a lemon twist.

Martini

(original, sweet)

- 2½ ounces (75ml) gin
- ¾ ounce (22ml) sweet vermouth
- Dash orange bitters

Stir with ice and strain into a cocktail glass.

Garnish with a cherry or lemon twist.

FLEISCHMANN'S MIXER'S MANUAL

1950S

Martini

(original, dry)

- 2½ ounces (75ml) gin
- ¾ ounce (22ml) dry vermouth
- Dash orange bitters

Stir with ice and strain into a cocktail glass.

Garnish with a lemon twist or olive.

Martini

(original, perfect)

- 2½ ounces (75ml) gin
- ½ ounce (15ml) sweet vermouth
- ½ ounce (15ml) dry vermouth
- Dash orange bitters

Stir with ice and strain into a cocktail glass.

Garnish with a lemon twist.

Martinez

Martini

(modern)

- 3 ounces (90ml) gin or vodka

Shake with ice.

Strain into a cocktail glass that has been rinsed with dry vermouth.

Garnish with several olives.

Metropole

- 1½ ounce (45ml) brandy
- 1½ ounce (45ml) dry vermouth
- 2 dashes orange bitters
- 1 dash Peychaud's bitters

Stir with ice and strain into a cocktail glass.

Garnish with a cherry.

Milk Punch

- 2 ounces (60ml) bourbon whiskey
- 4 ounces (120ml) milk
- ½ teaspoon (2ml) dark rum
- 1 tablespoon (15ml) simple syrup
- Nutmeg

Shake with ice.

Strain into a chilled 10-ounce (300ml) highball glass with a couple of ice cubes.

Dust with nutmeg.

Mimosa

- 2 ounces (60ml) orange juice
- 4 ounces (120ml) sparkling wine

Pour orange juice into a champagne flute or wine glass and then add the sparkling wine.

jones
complete
BARGUIDE

1977

Mint Julep

- 3 ounces (90ml) bourbon whiskey
- 4 to 6 sprigs of mint
- 1 ounce (30ml) simple syrup

Muddle the mint and simple syrup in the bottom of a rocks glass or, better yet, a silver mint julep cup.

Add the bourbon and stir to mix.

Fill with finely crushed ice and stir with a swizzle stick until ice begins to form on the outside of the cup.

Top with more crushed ice.

Garnish with a mint sprig and a sprinkle of powdered sugar.

Serve with straws.

It has become common to construct the Mint Julep with what might otherwise be referred to as a frappé process. Of course, there are a variety of other methods associated with this drink. Give this one a try, and if you like it, do a little research to find some of the various other methods and see which one you like the best.

Mix '06

(by Robert Hess, 2006)

- 1 ounce (30ml) gin
- ½ ounce (15ml) Bénédictine
- ¼ ounce (7ml) Campari
- 1 dash Peychaud's bitters
- Top with ginger ale

Shake everything with ice except the ginger ale.

Strain into an ice-filled Collins glass.

Top with ginger ale.

Garnish with a lime twist.

Mint Julep

Mojito

- 2 ounces (60ml) light rum
- 1 ounce (30ml) lime juice
- 2 teaspoons (10ml) sugar
- 4 to 6 sprigs of mint
- Club soda

Place the sugar, mint and a splash of club soda into a highball glass.

Using a muddler, lightly press the mint to extract the oils and dissolve the sugar.

Add the lime juice and rum.

Stir to combine.

Fill the glass with ice and stir to chill.

Top with club soda and garnish with a mint sprig and wedge of lime.

Monkey Gland

- 2 ounces (60ml) gin
- 1 ounce (30ml) orange juice
- ¼ ounce (7ml) grenadine
- 1 dash absinthe or pastis

Shake with ice and strain into a cocktail glass.

Garnish with an orange twist.

Monte Carlo

- 2¼ ounces (67ml) rye whiskey
- ¾ ounce (22ml) Bénédictine
- 1 dash Angostura bitters

Stir with ice and strain into a cocktail glass.

Mojito

Morning Cocktail

- 1½ ounce (45ml) brandy
- 1½ ounce (45ml) dry vermouth
- 2 dashes orange curaçao
- 2 dashes maraschino liqueur
- 2 dashes orange bitters
- 2 dashes absinthe or pastis

Stir with ice and strain into a cocktail glass.

Garnish with a cherry and lemon twist.

Morris Cocktail

(by Jamie Boudreau, for Vessel in Seattle, Washington)

- 1½ ounce (45ml) bourbon whiskey
- 1 ounce (30ml) Lillet Blanc
- ½ ounce (15ml) sweet vermouth
- 1 dash orange bitters
- 1 dash of simple syrup

Stir with ice and strain into a cocktail glass.

Garnish with an orange twist.

Jamie recommends using Woodford Reserve bourbon whiskey, Fee Brothers orange bitters and Amaro Nonino for the sweet vermouth.

Moscow Mule

Moscow Mule

- 2 ounces (60ml) vodka
- 3 ounces (90ml) ginger beer
- 1 ounce (30ml) lime juice

Build in an ice-filled highball glass or copper mug.

Garnish with a lime wedge.

Mother-In-Law

- 2 ounces (60ml) bourbon
- 1 teaspoon (5ml) Cointreau
- 1 teaspoon (5ml) maraschino liqueur
- 1 teaspoon (5ml) simple syrup
- 2 dashes Peychaud's bitters
- 2 dashes Angostura bitters
- 2 dashes Amer Picon

Stir with ice and strain into a cocktail glass.

Garnish with a cherry.

Naciónal

(by Francesco Lafranconi)

- 1½ ounce (45ml) rum
- 2 wedges of lime
- 2 dashes Angostura bitters
- Fresh mint
- 4 ounces (120ml) cola
- ½ ounce (15ml) amaretto

Muddle lime, mint and bitters in a highball glass.

Add ice and rum.

Fill with cola and then add a float of amaretto.

Garnish with a sprig of mint.

Francesco recommends using 10 Cane rum and Disaronno amaretto.

Negroni

- 1 ounce (30ml) gin
- 1 ounce (30ml) sweet vermouth
- 1 ounce (30ml) Campari

Stir with ice and strain into a cocktail glass. (It's not uncommon to strain the drink into an ice-filled rocks glass.)

Garnish with a lemon twist or an orange slice.

Negroni

Nicky Finn

- 1 ounce (30ml) brandy
- 1 ounce (30ml) Cointreau
- 1 ounce (30ml) lemon juice
- Dash absinthe or pastis

Shake with ice and strain into a cocktail glass.

Garnish with cherry or a lemon twist.

Nightwatch

(by Robert Hess, 2006)

- 1 ounce (30ml) gin
- 1 ounce (30ml) coffee liqueur
- ¼ ounce (7ml) absinthe or pastis

Shake with ice and strain into a cocktail glass.

Obituary Cocktail

- 2 ounces (60ml) gin
- ¼ ounce (7ml) dry vermouth
- ¼ ounce (7ml) absinthe or absinthe substitute

Stir with ice and strain into a cocktail glass.

Old Fashioned

Old Fashioned

- 1 sugar cube (1 teaspoon/ 5ml)
- 1 teaspoon (5ml) water
- 2 dashes Angostura bitters
- 2 ounces (60ml) American rye or bourbon whiskey

Muddle sugar, water and bitters together until the sugar is mostly dissolved.

Fill glass with ice, and then add the whiskey and stir briefly to chill.

Garnish with a twist of orange peel and a cherry.

Serve with straws.

Old Hickory

- 1 ounce (30ml) dry vermouth
- 1 ounce (30ml) sweet vermouth
- 1 dash orange bitters
- 2 dashes Peychaud's bitters

Stir with ice and strain into a cocktail glass.

Garnish with a lemon twist.

Old Pal

- 1½ ounce (45ml) rye or bourbon whiskey
- ¾ ounce (22ml) dry vermouth
- ¾ ounce (22ml) Campari

Stir with ice and strain into a cocktail glass.

Garnish with a lemon twist.

Opera

- 2 ounces (60ml) gin
- ½ ounce (15ml) Dubonnet rouge
- ¼ ounce (7ml) maraschino liqueur
- 1 dash orange bitters

Stir with ice and strain into a cocktail glass.

Garnish with a lemon twist.

1930

Palm Beach Special

- 2 ounces (60ml) gin
- ½ ounce (15ml) sweet vermouth
- ½ ounce (15ml) grapefruit juice

Shake with ice and strain into a cocktail glass.

Parisian

- 1½ ounce (45ml) gin
- 1½ ounce (45ml) dry vermouth
- ½ ounce (15ml) crème de cassis

Stir with ice and strain into a cocktail glass.

Garnish with a lemon twist.

Park Avenue

- 2 ounces (60ml) gin
- 1 ounce (30ml) pineapple juice
- ½ ounce (15ml) sweet vermouth
- Dash orange curaçao

Shake with ice.

Strain into a cocktail glass.

Parkside Fizz

(by Jim Meehan, for PDT in New York)

- 2 ounces (60ml) citrus vodka
- ¾ ounce (22ml) lemon juice
- ½ ounce (30ml) orgeat (almond syrup)
- 6-8 mint leaves
- 1 ounce (30ml) club soda

Muddle the mint and orgeat in a mixing glass.

Add all but the club soda and shake with ice.

Strain into an ice-filled rocks glass.

Top with club soda and garnish with a mint sprig.

Jim recommends using Hangar One Buddha's Hand for the vodka in this drink.

Pegu

- 2 ounces (60ml) gin
- 1 ounce (30ml) orange curaçao
- 1 teaspoon (5 ml) lime juice
- 1 dash Angostura bitters
- 1 dash orange bitters

Shake with ice and strain into a cocktail glass.

Garnish with a lime wedge.

Pegu

Pepper Delirious

(by Ryan Magarian)

- 2 thin yellow bell pepper rings
- ⅔ cup (40g) loosely packed mint
- 2 ounces (60ml) gin
- ¾ ounce (22ml) lemon juice
- ¾ ounce (22ml) simple syrup

Muddle everything together in a mixing glass without ice.

Shake with ice and strain into a cocktail glass.

Garnish with a mint sprig and thin ring of yellow pepper.

Ryan recommends using Aviation gin to make this drink.

Petit Zinc

(by Paul Harrington)

- 1 ounce (30ml) vodka
- ½ ounce (15ml) Cointreau
- ½ ounce (15ml) sweet vermouth
- ½ ounce (15ml) orange juice (use fresh-squeezed Seville oranges; if not available, add ¼ ounce (7ml) lemon juice to recipe).

Shake with ice and strain into a cocktail glass.

Garnish with a wedge of orange.

Paul came up with this recipe trying to recreate a drink one of his customers remembers having on a trip to Paris.

Picon Cremaillere

- 1½ ounce (45ml) gin
- ¾ ounce (22ml) Amer Picon
- ¾ ounce (22ml) Dubonnet rouge
- 1 dash orange bitters

Stir with ice and strain into a cocktail glass.

Picon Punch

- 2 ounces (60ml) Amer Picon
- ½ ounce (15ml) lemon juice
- ½ ounce (15ml) grenadine
- 4 ounces (120ml) club soda

Shake the Amer Picon, lemon juice and grenadine with ice.

Strain into an ice-filled highball glass.

Top with club soda.

Garnish with seasonal fruits.

Pepper Delirious

Pimm's Cup

Pimm's Cup

- 2 ounces (60ml) Pimm's No. 1
- 3 ounces (90ml) ginger ale
- Cucumber

Pour Pimm's into a highball glass.

Fill with ice and top with ginger ale or lemon/lime soda.

Garnish with a wedge of lemon and a slice of cucumber.

Pina Colada

Piña Colada

- 2 ounces (60ml) white rum
- 1 ounce (30ml) coconut cream
- 1 ounce (30ml) heavy cream
- 6 ounces (180ml) pineapple juice
- 4 ounces (120ml) crushed ice

Blend all ingredients with crushed ice until it just reaches a smooth consistency.

Pour into a wine goblet and garnish with pineapple spear and cherry.

Piña Partida

(by Junior Merino)

- 2 chunks pineapple
- 2 slices cucumber
- 3 lemon wedges
- ⅓ ounce (10ml) simple syrup
- 1½ ounce (45ml) silver tequila
- ½ ounce (15ml) lemon/lime soda

Muddle the pineapple, cucumber, lemon and simple syrup.

Add the tequila and shake with ice.

Strain into an ice-filled highball glass and top with lemon/lime soda.

Garnish with a slice of cucumber.

Pink Gin

- 1½ ounce (45ml) gin
- 3 or 4 dashes Angostura bitters

Stir with ice and strain into a cocktail glass.

Pink Gin and Tonic

*(by Dale DeGroff,
for Plymouth Gin)*

- 1½ ounce (45ml) Plymouth Gin
- 2 dashes Peychaud's bitters
- 2 sage leaves
- 4 ounces (120ml) tonic water

Lightly muddle sage leaves in the bottom of a highball glass.

Fill the glass with ice.

Add the gin, bitters and tonic water.

Stir briefly.

Dale recommends using Plymouth for the gin and a high quality tonic water (Schweppes or Fever Tree).

Pink Lady

- 1½ ounce (45ml) gin
- ½ ounce (15ml) applejack
- ¾ ounce (22ml) lemon juice
- ¼ ounce (7ml) grenadine
- 1 egg white

Shake with ice and strain into a wine glass.

Pisco Sour

- 2¼ ounce (67ml) pisco
- ¾ ounce (22ml) lime juice
- ¾ ounce (22ml) simple syrup
- 1 whole egg white
- Several dashes Angostura bitters.

Shake hard with ice to build up a good foam.

Strain into a flute or sour glass.

Use the bitters as an aromatic garnish to top the finished drink.

Garnish with an orange slice and cherry.

Like all punch drinks, topping with club soda is optional.

If you try to find the definitive recipe for a Planters Punch, you might drive yourself to drink. This is just one of many variations.

Pisco Sour

Poet's Dream

- ¾ ounce (22ml) gin
- ¾ ounce (22ml) dry vermouth
- ¾ ounce (22ml) Bénédictine

Planters Punch

- 1 ounce (30ml) dark rum
- 1 ounce (30ml) light rum
- ½ ounce (15ml) orange curaçao
- 2 ounces (60ml) orange juice
- 2 ounces (60ml) pineapple juice
- ½ ounce (15ml) simple syrup
- ¼ ounce (7ml) lime juice
- 1 dash grenadine
- 1 dash Angostura bitters

Shake all ingredients well with ice and strain into an iced Collins glass.

Top with a small amount of club soda.

Stir with ice and strain into a cocktail glass.

Garnish with a lemon twist.

Port Wine Cocktail

- 2 ounces (60ml) ruby port
- Dash brandy

Stir with ice and strain into a cocktail glass.

Garnish with a lemon twist.

Precious Thyme

(by Francesco Lafranconi)

- 1 ounce (30ml) Campari
- 1 ounce (30ml) limoncello
- 1 ounce (30ml) sweet vermouth
- 2 ounces (60ml) club soda
- 1 sprig of fresh thyme

Pour ingredients into an ice-filled highball glass and stir.

Garnish with the thyme, an orange slice and a lemon twist.

Pusser's Painkiller

(by Charles Tobias, for Pusser's Rum)

- 2 ounces (60ml) Pusser's rum
- 4 ounces (120ml) unsweetened pineapple juice
- 1 ounce (30ml) orange juice
- 1 ounce (30ml) coconut cream

Shake with ice and strain into an ice-filled Collins glass or Tiki mug.

Garnish with ground nutmeg, cinnamon, pineapple stick and orange wheel.

Ramos Gin Fizz

- 2 ounces (60ml) gin
- 1 ounce (30ml) cream
- 1 whole egg white
- ½ ounce (15ml) lemon juice
- ½ ounce (15ml) lime juice
- 1¼ ounce (37ml) simple syrup
- 2 dashes orange flower water
- 1 ounce (30ml) club soda

Minus the club soda and without ice, shake all ingredients very hard to quicken the emulsification.

Add ice and shake some more (at least a minute), resulting in a fairly foamy consistency. Strain into a Collins glass with a few cubes of ice and top with the club soda.

Red Snapper

- 2 ounces (60ml) gin
- 4 ounces (120ml) tomato juice
- ½ ounce (15ml) lemon juice
- Pinch of salt and pepper
- 2 to 3 dashes Worcestershire sauce
- 2 to 3 drops Tabasco sauce

Stir all ingredients with ice in a highball glass.

Garnish with a celery stalk and a lemon wedge.

The Reluctant Tabby Cat

(by Gary Regan)

- 1¼ ounces (37ml) Dubonnet rouge
- ½ ounce (15ml) limoncello
- ¼ ounce (7ml) Scotch whisky

Shake with ice and strain into a wine goblet.

Garnish with a lemon twist.

Gary recommends using Pallini Limoncello and Laphroaig Single Malt Scotch for this drink.

Remsen Cooler

- 2 ounces (60ml) Scotch whisky
- 4 ounces (120ml) club soda

Garnish a Collins glass with a long and wide spiral of lemon peel (try to peel the whole lemon in one long spiral about ³/₄ inch/19mm wide), with the spiral hanging partially out of the glass.

Add a few ice cubes and then the scotch.

Top with club soda.

Renaissance

(by Robert Hess, 2002)

- 2 ounces (60ml) brandy
- 1 ounce (30ml) sweet vermouth
- ¼ ounce (7ml) limoncello
- 2 dashes peach bitters

Stir with ice and train into a cocktail glass.

Garnish with a lemon twist.

I created this drink to focus on an Italian angle with the sweet vermouth and limoncello as well as to experiment with peach bitters.

1940s

Retreat

(by David Nepove, 1st place in StarChef.com cocktail competition)

- 1 ounce (30ml) lemon juice
- ½ ounce (15ml) simple syrup
- 5 basil leaves
- 1½ ounce (45ml) citrus vodka
- ½ ounce (15ml) Pernod
- 2 ounces (60ml) club soda

Muddle the basil in lemon juice and simple syrup.

Add vodka and the Pernod and shake with ice.

Double strain into an ice-filled Collins glass and top with club soda.

Garnish with a sprig of basil and a lemon twist.

David uses Absolut Citron for this drink.

Robert Burns

- 2¼ ounce (67ml) Scotch whisky
- ¾ ounce (22ml) sweet vermouth
- 1 dash orange bitters
- 1 dash absinthe or pastis

Stir with ice and strain into a cocktail glass.

Rob Roy

- 2¼ ounce (67ml) Scotch whisky
- ¾ ounce (22ml) sweet vermouth
- 1 dash orange bitters

Stir with ice and strain into a cocktail glass.

Garnish with lemon twist.

This is essentially a Manhattan made with Scotch whisky instead of American. Like a Manhattan, it can be made with Angostura bitters instead of orange.

Rob Roy

Rose

- 2 ounces (60ml) dry vermouth
- 1 ounce (30ml) kirschwasser
- 1 teaspoon (5ml) raspberry or red currant syrup

Stir with ice and strain into a cocktail glass.

Garnish with a cherry.

Rosita

- 1½ ounce (45ml) silver tequila
- ½ ounce (15ml) sweet vermouth
- ½ ounce (15ml) dry vermouth
- ½ ounce (15ml) Campari
- 1 dash Angostura bitters

Stir with ice and strain into an ice-filled rocks glass.

Garnish with lemon twist.

This is an excellent cocktail to celebrate, rather than mask, the flavor of tequila. Unfortunately, it is rarely seen in cocktail manuals.

Rubicon

(by Jamie Boudreau, for Vessel in Seattle)

- ½ ounce (15ml) green Chartreuse
- 1 rosemary sprig
- 2 ounces (60ml) gin
- ½ ounce (15ml) maraschino liqueur
- ½ ounce (15ml) lemon juice

Curl the rosemary sprig into the bottom of a rocks glass.

Add the Chartreuse.

Light the Chartreuse and allow to burn while you mix the drink.

Shake the gin, maraschino liqueur and lemon juice with ice.

Strain into the glass to extinguish the flame.

Top with crushed ice.

"For a little added flare, I keep some Chartreuse in a fancy misting bottle, and use this as a torch to light the chartreuse by holding a match in front of the nozzle."
Jamie Boudreau

Rubicon

Rusty Nail

- 1½ ounce (45ml) Scotch whisky
- ½ ounce (15ml) Drambuie

Stir with ice and strain into an ice-filled rocks glass.

Saratoga

- ¾ ounce (22ml) brandy
- ¾ ounce (22ml) rye whiskey
- ¾ ounce (22ml) sweet vermouth
- 2 dashes Angostura bitters

Stir with ice and strain into a cocktail glass.

Garnish with a slice of lemon.

Satan's Whiskers

- ¾ ounce (22ml) gin
- ¾ ounce (22ml) dry vermouth
- ¾ ounce (22ml) sweet vermouth
- ½ ounce (15ml) orange juice
- ½ ounce (15ml) Grand Marnier
- 1 dash orange bitters

Shake with ice and strain into a cocktail glass.

You can use orange curaçao instead of Grand Marnier in which case this would be *curled*.

Sazerac

- 1 sugar cube (1 teaspoon/5ml)
- 1 teaspoon (5ml) water
- 2 dashes Peychaud's bitters
- 3 ounces (90ml) rye whiskey
- 1 teaspoon (5ml) absinthe or absinthe substitute

Prepare a small rocks glass by coating it with absinthe.

Put the sugar, water and bitters into a mixing glass and muddle to dissolve the sugar and form a syrup.

Add the rye to the mixing glass and fill the glass with ice and stir.

Strain into the rocks glass.

Garnish with a lemon twist.

Variation: You can use simple syrup instead of the sugar cube and water to avoid undissolved sugar remaining in the drink.

Sazerac

Scofflaw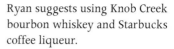

- 1 ounce (30ml) Canadian whisky
- 1 ounce (30ml) dry vermouth
- ¼ ounce (7ml) lemon juice
- Dash of grenadine
- Dash of orange bitters

Stir with ice and strain into a cocktail glass.

Garnish with a lemon wedge.

Scottish Guard

- 1½ ounce (45ml) bourbon whiskey
- ½ ounce (15ml) lemon juice
- ½ ounce (15ml) orange juice
- 1 teaspoon (5ml) grenadine

Shake with ice and strain into a cocktail glass.

Seattle Manhattan

(by Ryan Magarian)

- 2 ounces (60ml) bourbon whiskey
- ½ ounce (15ml) sweet vermouth
- ½ ounce (15ml) coffee liqueur

Stir with ice and strain into a cocktail glass.

Garnish with three coffee beans.

Ryan suggests using Knob Creek bourbon whiskey and Starbucks coffee liqueur.

"I created this for the launch of Starbucks Coffee Liqueur."

-Ryan Magarian

Sidecar

- 2 ounces (60ml) brandy (cognac)
- 1 ounce (30ml) Cointreau
- ½ ounce (15ml) lemon juice

Shake with ice and strain into cocktail glass.

Sugar, while not part of the original recipe, is commonly used to rim the glass. I think this just leaves you with sticky fingers.

1922

Silk Stockings

- 1 ounce (30ml) tequila
- ¾ ounce (22ml) white crème de cacao
- ¾ ounce (22ml) cream
- Dash of grenadine

Shake hard with ice to froth the cream a little.

Strain into a cocktail glass.

Garnish with a sprinkle of nutmeg.

Without the grenadine this would be a Frostbite.

Singapore Sling

- 1½ ounce (45ml) gin
- ½ ounce (15ml) Cherry Heering Liqueur
- ¼ ounce (7ml) Cointreau
- ¼ ounce (7ml) Bénédictine
- 4 ounces (120ml) pineapple juice
- ½ ounce (15ml) lime juice
- ⅓ ounce (10ml) grenadine
- Dash bitters

Shake with ice and strain into an ice-filled Collins glass.

Garnish with cherry and slice of pineapple.

Southside

- 1½ ounce (45ml) gin
- ¾ ounce (22ml) lemon juice
- ½ ounce (15ml) simple syrup

Shake with ice and strain into a cocktail glass.

Garnish with mint sprigs.

Thought to have originated in Prohibition Chicago, this drink was possibly created as a way for Southside mobsters to drink their rather cheap gin. Northside gangsters preferred to mix their gin with ginger ale for the same purpose.

Spanish Bay

(by Chris Hannah, for Arnaud's French 75 bar in New Orleans)

- 1 ounce (30ml) sherry
- 1 ounce (30ml) green Chartreuse
- 1 ounce (30ml) orange juice

Shake with ice and strain into a cocktail glass.

Chris recommends using Dry Sack sherry.

Spanish Rose

(by David Nepove)

- 1½ ounce (45ml) gin
- ¾ ounce (22ml) Licor 43
- ½ ounce (15ml) lemon juice
- ¼ ounce (7ml) cranberry juice
- 1 sprig rosemary

Muddle half of the rosemary sprig in the lemon juice and Licor 43.

Add the gin and shake with ice.

Double strain into an ice-filled Collins glass.

Add the cranberry juice.

Garnish with the other half of rosemary.

Stargazer

(by Robert Hess, 2006)

- 1½ ounce (45ml) rye whiskey
- 1½ ounce (45ml) Lillet Blanc
- 1 dash Angostura bitters

Stir with ice and strain into a cocktail glass.

Garnish with a lemon twist.

Stinger

- 1 ounce (30ml) brandy
- ¼ ounce (7ml) crème de menthe (white)

Stir with ice and strain into a cocktail glass.

Garnish with fresh sprigs of mint, and serve with a glass of ice water.

1927

The Stork Club Bar Book

Lucius Beebe

1946

Stork Club

- 1½ ounce (45ml) gin
- ½ ounce (15ml) Cointreau
- 1 ounce (30ml) orange juice
- ¼ ounce (7ml) lime juice
- 1 dash Angostura bitters

Shake with ice and strain into a cocktail glass.

Garnish with an orange peel.

Straits Sling

- 2 ounces (60ml) gin
- ½ ounce (15ml) dry cherry brandy
- ½ ounce (15ml) Bénédictine
- 1 ounce (30ml) lemon juice
- 2 dashes of orange bitters
- 2 dashes of Angostura bitters

Shake with ice and strain into an ice-filled Collins glass.

Fill with club soda.

Strega Daiquiri

- 1 ounce (30ml) light rum
- 1 ounce (30ml) Strega
- ½ ounce (15ml) lemon juice
- ½ ounce (15ml) orange juice
- ½ teaspoon (2.5ml) orgeat (almond syrup)

Shake with ice and strain into a cocktail glass.

Garnish with a cherry.

Strega is an Italian liqueur that is often hard to find, but it has an excellent complex slightly sweet flavor.

Sweet Heat

(by David Nepove, 1st place Gran Centenario Cocktail Competition, 2002)

- 2 ounces (60ml) tequila
- ½ jalapeño (with seeds removed)
- 1 ounce (30ml) lime juice
- 1 ounce (30ml) simple syrup
- 1 ounce (30ml) Licor 43

Muddle the jalapeño in the lime juice and simple syrup.

Add the tequila and shake with ice.

Strain into an ice-filled Collins glass.

Garnish with a lime wheel.

Tailspin

- ¾ ounce (22ml) gin
- ¾ ounce (22ml) sweet vermouth
- ¾ ounce (22ml) green Chartreuse
- 1 dash Campari

Stir with ice and strain into a cocktail glass.

Garnish with lemon twist and cherry.

Tango

- ½ ounce (15ml) rum
- ½ ounce (15ml) sweet vermouth
- ½ ounce (15ml) dry vermouth
- ½ ounce (15ml) Bénédictine
- ½ ounce (15ml) orange juice

Shake with ice and strain into a cocktail glass.

Garnish with an orange twist.

Ti Punch

- 1½ ounce (45ml) rum
- ¼ ounce (7ml) simple syrup
- Thin slice of lime peel

Add everything to a small rocks glass with a small piece of ice.

Stir and serve.

Traditionally this would be made with rhum agricole, which is a rum made from sugar instead of molasses.

Tillicum

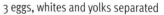

(by Robert Hess)

- 2¼ ounces (67ml) gin
- ¾ ounce (22ml) dry vermouth
- 2 dashes Peychaud's bitters

Stir with ice and strain into a cocktail glass.

Garnish with a slice of raw smoked salmon skewered flat on a pick.

I created this drink while playing around with Martinis that used different garnishes. The name comes from the traditional way Indians from Tillicum Village would prepare their salmon for cooking around the fire. This is reflected in the salmon garnish.

Tip Top

- 2 ounces (60ml) dry vermouth
- ¼ ounce (7ml) Bénédictine
- 2 dashes Angostura bitters

Stir with ice and strain into a cocktail glass.

Garnish with a lemon twist.

Tom and Jerry

Batter mix:

3 eggs, whites and yolks separated
- ½ ounce (15ml) rum
- ½ teaspoon (2.5ml) cinnamon
- Dash cloves
- Dash allspice
- Dash cream of tartar
- Dash vanilla
- ½ cup (115g) sugar

In one bowl, beat the egg whites to a stiff froth.

In another bowl, beat the yolks until they are as thin as water.

Mix yolks and whites together and add the rum and spices.

Thicken with sugar until the mixture attains the consistence of a light batter.

For each drink, combine in a coffee mug one tablespoonful of the mixture and 2 ounces (60ml) of brandy. Then fill the glass with boiling water or, better yet, steamed milk.

Garnish by grating a little nutmeg on top.

Tillicum

Tom Collins

- 2 ounces (60ml) gin
- ¾ ounce (22ml) lemon juice
- 1 teaspoon (5ml) superfine sugar or simple syrup
- 2 ounces (60ml) club soda

Shake with ice and strain into an ice-filled Collins glass.

Top with club soda and garnish with a cherry and orange wheel.

Trident

(by Robert Hess, 2002)

- 1 ounce (30ml) dry sherry
- 1 ounce (30ml) Cynar
- 1 ounce (30ml) aquavit
- 2 dashes peach bitters

Stir with ice and strain into a cocktail glass.

Garnish with a lemon twist.

Trident

Twentieth Century Cocktail

- 1½ ounce (45ml) gin
- ¾ ounce (22ml) Lillet Blanc
- ¾ ounce (22ml) lemon juice
- ½ ounce (15ml) white crème de cacao

Shake with ice and strain into a cocktail glass.

Twenty-first Century Cocktail

(by Jim Meehan, for PDT in New York)

- 1½ ounce (45ml) silver or blanco tequila
- ¾ ounce (22ml) white crème de cacao
- ¾ ounce (22ml) lemon juice
- ¼ ounce (7ml) absinthe or pastis

Prepare a cocktail glass by pouring in the absinthe or pastis, then swirl to coat and dump the liquid.

Shake everything else with ice and strain into the prepared cocktail glass.

Jim recommends using Herradura or Partida tequila and Marie Brizard crème de cacao.

Tyrol

- ½ ounce (15ml) brandy
- ½ ounce (15ml) green Chartreuse
- 1 ounce (30ml) Galliano
- ½ ounce (15ml) cream

Shake with ice and strain into a cocktail glass.

Garnish with nutmeg.

Union Club

(by Jamie Boudreau, for Vessel in Seattle)

- 2 ounces (60ml) bourbon whiskey
- ½ ounce (15ml) maraschino liqueur
- ½ ounce (15ml) Campari
- 1½ ounce (45ml) orange juice

Shake with ice and strain into a cocktail glass.

Union Club

Velvet Harvest

Velvet Harvest

(by Chad Solomon)

- 2 ounces (60ml) pear brandy
- ½ ounce (15ml) falernum
- ½ ounce (15ml) apple schnapps
- ¼ ounce (7ml) maple syrup
- ½ ounce (15ml) lemon juice
- 1 egg white
- 2 dashes Angostura bitters
- 2 dashes clove tincture*

Shake vigorously with ice to emulsify the egg white and then strain into a cocktail glass.

Garnish with 3 additional drops of clove tincture and a pear slice.

*clove tincture- combine 1 ounce (30g) of whole cloves and 8 ounces (240ml) of vodka in a glass container and seal. Let infuse for two weeks, and then strain into a dasher bottle.

Chad recommends using Clear Creek Poire Eau de Vie for the pear brandy and Velvet Falernum.

Vesper

- 3 ounces (90ml) gin
- 1 ounce (30ml) vodka
- ½ ounce (15ml) Lillet Blanc

Stir with ice and strain into a cocktail glass.

Garnish with lemon twist.

Angostura Bitters, 1900

Vieux Carré

- ¾ ounce (22ml) rye whiskey
- ¾ ounce (22ml) brandy
- ¾ ounce (22ml) sweet vermouth
- ¼ ounce (7ml) Bénédictine
- 1 dash Peychaud's bitters
- 1 dash Angostura bitters

Build over ice in a rocks glass.

Garnish with a lemon twist.

Voyager

(by Robert Hess, 2006)

- 2 ounces (60ml) rum
- ½ ounce (15ml) lime juice
- ½ ounce (15ml) Bénédictine
- ½ ounce (15ml) falernum
- 2 dashes Angostura bitters

Shake with ice and strain into an ice-filled rocks glass.

Garnish with a lime wedge.

This represents my entry into the classic Tiki cocktail arena. Back in those days, the Polynesian inspired restaurants were intended as a mini-vacation, hence the Voyager name. That, and the fact that I'm also a *Star Trek* fan.

Ward 8

- 2 ounces (60ml) rye whiskey
- ½ ounce (15ml) lemon juice
- ½ ounce (15ml) orange juice
- 1 teaspoon (5ml) grenadine

Shake with ice and strain into a cocktail glass.

Whiskey Sour

- 2 ounces (60ml) bourbon whiskey
- 1 ounce (30ml) simple syrup
- ¾ ounce (22ml) lemon juice
- 1 teaspoon (5ml) egg white (optional)

Shake with ice and strain into a small rocks glass or a small wine glass.

This is perhaps the quintessential drink in the sour category. The optional bit of egg white adds a bit of texture as well as a slightly foamy head. Once there was a common sour glass used for this drink. It looked like a cross between a small wine glass and a champagne flute.

Whiskey Sour

White Spider

- 1 ounce (30ml) gin
- 1 ounce (30ml) lemon juice
- ½ ounce (15ml) Cointreau
- 1 teaspoon (5ml) simple syrup

Shake with ice and strain into a cocktail glass.

Widow's Kiss

- 2 ounces (60ml) calvados or apple brandy
- 1 ounce (30ml) yellow Chartreuse
- 1 ounce (30ml) Bénédictine
- 1 dash Angostura bitters

Stir with ice and strain into a cocktail glass.

White Lady

- 2 ounces (60ml) gin
- 1 ounce (30ml) Cointreau
- ½ ounce (15ml) lemon juice

Shake with ice and strain into a cocktail glass.

White Russian

- 2 ounces (60ml) vodka
- 1 ounce (30ml) coffee liqueur
- ½ ounce (15ml) cream

Pour vodka and coffee liqueur over ice into a rocks glass, then float cream on top.

This is the same as a Black Russian, except with the addition of the float of cream.

White Russian

Xeres

- 2 ounces (60ml) sherry
- 1 dash orange bitters
- 1 dash peach bitters

Stir with ice and strain into a cocktail glass.

X.Y.Z.

- 2 ounces (60ml) rum
- 1 ounce (30ml) Cointreau
- ½ ounce (15ml) lemon juice

Shake with ice and strain into a cocktail glass.

Yacht Club

- ¾ ounce (22ml) gin
- ¾ ounce (22ml) sweet vermouth
- ¾ ounce (22ml) orange juice
- 2 dashes Campari
- 2 dashes simple syrup

Shake with ice and strain into a cocktail glass.

1942

Zaza

- ¾ ounce (22ml) gin
- 1½ ounce (45ml) Dubonnet rouge
- 1 dash orange bitters

Stir with ice and strain into a cocktail glass.

This drink most likely dates from around 1900. There was a popular French play at the time called *Zaza* (short for Isabelle), which became both an opera and a film.

Zombie

(Created by Don the Beachcomber)

- 1 ounce (30ml) lemon juice
- 1 ounce (30ml) lime juice
- 1 ounce (30ml) pineapple juice
- 1 teaspoon (5ml) brown sugar
- 1 ounce (30ml) passion fruit syrup
- 1 dash Angostura bitters
- 1 ounce (30ml) gold rum
- 1 ounce (30ml) 151 Demerara rum
- 1 ounce (30ml) white rum

Dissolve sugar in juice.

Shake with ice and pour into a Collins glass.

Garnish with a mint sprig.

1942

1961

Zumbo

- 1½ ounce (45ml) gin
- ¼ ounce (7ml) Cointreau
- ¼ ounce (7ml) sweet vermouth
- ¼ ounce (7ml) dry vermouth
- 2 dashes Fernet Branca

Stir with ice and strain into a cocktail glass.

Zummy

- ¾ ounce (22ml) Bénédictine
- ¾ ounce (22ml) gin
- ½ ounce (15ml) dry vermouth
- ½ ounce (15ml) sweet vermouth
- 1 dash Campari

Stir with ice and strain into a cocktail glass.

Measurement Equivalents

Throughout the recipes in this book I have attempted to use U.S. ounces for all measurements (with English milliliter equivalents), and the odd teaspoon or tablespoon thrown in when that was appropriate for the product being measured. However, there might be times that you will need to convert these measures to something else, or you might come across other recipes which you want to convert to ounces and such. Here are some handy conversion details.

ODD MEASURES:

1 jigger = $1^{1}/_{2}$ ounces

1 pony = 1 ounce

1 shot = 1 ounce

1 wineglass = 2 ounces (often used in recipes in the 1800s)

1 drink = $1^{1}/_{2}$ to 2 ounces

1 dash = $^{1}/_{70}$th ounce (approximate)

1 drop = $^{1}/_{456}$th ounce (approximate)

1 lemon = $1^{1}/_{2}$ ounces (average)

1 lime = 1 ounce (average)

1 orange = $2^{3}/_{4}$ ounce (average)

1 splash = unknown quantity, use should be avoided

You will also sometimes see *part* used in cocktail recipes. This is intended as a flexible unit of measure in which the ratios of the ingredients are being specified (i.e.: 1 part vermouth, 3 parts gin, 1 dash orange bitters). A recipe using parts should never include specific measurements (ounce, tablespoon, etc), since that wouldn't make sense.

COMMON MEASURES:

1 oz = 6 teaspoons

1 oz = 2 Tablespoons

1 cup = 8 ounces

1 pint = 16 ounces

METRIC MEASURES *(APPROXIMATE)*:

$^{1}/_{4}$ ounce = 7ml

$^{1}/_{2}$ ounce = 15 ml

$^{3}/_{4}$ ounce = 22ml

1 ounce = 30ml

Bibliography

Bergeron, Victor, *Bartender's Guide*, Garden City, 1947

Berry, Jeff, *Sippin' Safari*, Club Tiki Press, 2007

Blue, Anthony, *The Complete Book of Spirits*, Harper Collins, 2004

Boothby, William, *American Bar-Tender*, San Francisco News Company, 1900

Brown, Lorraine, *The Story of Canadian Whiskey*, Fitzhenry & Whiteside, 1994

Calabrese, Salvatore, *Classic Cocktails*, Sterling Publishing, 1997

Difford, Simon, *Cocktails*, diffordsguide, 2005

Embury, David, *The Fine Art of Mixing Drinks*, Doubleday, 1948

Felten, Eric, *How's Your Drink?*, Surrey, 2007

Giglio, Anthony, *Mr. Boston's Platinum Bartender's Guide*, Wiley, 2006

Grossman, Harold, *Grossman's Guide to Wine*, Spirits, and Beers, Charles Scribner's Sons, 1940

Haigh, Ted, *Vintage Spirits & Forgotten Cocktails*, Rockport, 2004

Hess, Robert and Miller, Anistatia, *The Museum of the American Cocktail Pocket Recipe Guide*, Mixellany Press, 2006

Johnson, Harry, *New and Improved Bartender's Manual*, 1900

Jones, Stan, *Jones' Complete Barguide*, Barguide Enterprises, 1977

Lipinski, Robert & Kathleen, *Professional Guide to Alcoholic Beverages*, Van Nostrand Reinhold, 1989

McCaffety, Kerri, *Obituary Cocktail*, Winter Books, 1998

O'Hara, Christopher, *The Bloody Mary*, Lyons Press, 1999

Regan, Gary, *The Joy of Mixology*, Clarkson Potter, 2003

Regan, Gary & Mardee Haidin, *New Classic Cocktails*, Macmillian, 1997

Regan, Gary & Mardee Haidin, *The Book of Bourbon*, Chapters, 1995

Regan, Mardee Haidin, *The Bartender's Best Friend*, Wiley, 2003

Rothbaum, Noah, *The Business of Spirits*, Kaplan, 2007

Thomas, Jerry, *Bartender's Guide*, Dick & Fitzgerald, 1887

Thomas, Jerry, *How To Mix Drinks*, Dick & Fitzgerald, 1862

Wondrich, David, *Imbibe*, Perigree, 2007

Acknowledgements

The author would like to thank everybody who made this book possible. It was a great experience and a wonderful opportunity to be able to pull together all the information necessary to produce this book. Thanks have to start with Gregory Boehm who first envisioned this project and was at the heart of it from the very start. A large component of this book, of course, are the wonderful pictures and illustrations which bring life to its pages. For these I thank Chad Solomon and Christy Pope who painstakingly prepared the cocktails to be wonderfully photographed by Amy K. Sims. Scattered throughout the recipes are also unique creations by many of my cocktailian friends and co-workers around the world: Tony Abou-Ganim, Jamie Boudreau, Kathy Casey, Tito Class, Dale DeGroff, Chris Hannah, Paul Harrington, Bastian Heuser, Francesco Lafranconi, Ryan Magarian, Jim Meehan, Junior Merino, Sean Muldoon, David Nepove, Jonathan Pogash, Gary Regan, Mardee Regan, Charles Schumann, Laurel Semmes, Chad Solomon, Murray Stenson, Gwydion Stone, Chuck Taggart and Charles Tobias.

And I want to specifically thank those people who have specifically been instrumental along my own personal cocktailian journey: Paul Harrington, Ted "Dr. Cocktail" Haigh, Gary Regan, Mardee Haidin Regan, Jason Crume, Kacy Fitch, Ben Dougherty, Murray Stenson, Ryan Magarian, Dale DeGroff, Audrey Saunders, David Wondrich, Chris McMillan, Anistatia Miller, Jared Brown, Cheryl Charming, Simon Ford and Ann Tuennerman.

Photo Credits

Amy K. Sims (pages 31, 32, 64, 66, 69, 71, 72, 75, 77, 78, 87, 90, 93, 98, 104, 107, 109, 117, 122, 135, 141, 143, 146, 149, 156, 163, 164, 166, 169)

F. William Lagaret (pages 14, bottom; 18-22, 30, 35, 44, 49, 51, 53, 57, 59, 61, 85, 112, 122, 132, 139)

Ryan Magarian (pages 89, 110, 145)

Jamie Boudreau (pages 14, top; 16, 154, 165)

Greg Boehm (pages 115, 152)

Corbis Images: © Helen King/Corbis (page 9); Bettmann/CORBIS, January 9, 1951, Chicago, IL, USA (page 15)

Getty Images: Julien Capmeil (page 6)

istockphoto: Felipe Bello (page 45); Joe Biafore (page 34); Eugene Bochkarev (page 147); Chelsea Elizabeth Photography (page 92); John Clines (page 137); Danny Hooks (page 96); indykb (page 47); JackJelly (page 140); Zoran Kolundzija (page 62 (bottom left)); Ivan Mateev (pages 94, 103, 111, 123); Steven Miric (page 38); objectsforall (page 169); Philip Pellat (page 119); George Peters (page 39); Angel Rodríguez (page 138); Gary Sludden (page 126); David Smith (page 133); Klaudia Steiner (pages 62, 113); Daniel Timiraos (page 40); Montage, page 42: (Row 1, from left) Scott Waite, Larry White, Kevin Russ; (Row 2, from left) Michael Braun, Les Kollegian, Darla Hallmark; (Row 3) David Cannings-Bushell; (Row 4, from left) Mark Wilkinson, Anthony Hall

Jupiter Images: Aladdin Color Inc. (page 173)

StockFood: Cynthia Brown (page 81); Giblin - StockFood Munich (page 10); Amy K. Sims (page 82)

General Index

Index of Recipes by Main Alcoholic Ingredients

C

W

About the Author

Robert Hess lives and works in Seattle, Washington. He traces his interest in the cocktail to a childhood fascination of bartenders, who effortlessly transformed the contents of the bottles around them into gleaming jewels of refreshment. Eventually, he took action on these early memories, absorbing all he could about the classic art of mixology. Using his culinary training as a canvas, he views cocktails as a cuisine with the same artistic flavor potentials as the food prepared by a gourmet French chef. He has since become a ceaseless evangelist of quality cocktails, working with restaurants, bartenders and consumers to help them better understand how to advance their craft.

He created DrinkBoy.com and its associated discussion forum to allow bartenders around the world to interact with each other and share any thoughts, ideas and experiences that would benefit everybody through an open discussion. He has since teamed up with several others across the country to found The Museum of the American Cocktail (www.MuseumOfTheAmericanCocktail.org). Coinciding with the Museum's opening exhibits in New Orleans and New York will be a variety of events and seminars around the world.

He also is the host and executive producer of *The Cocktail Spirit* a web-based video series being presented through the Small Screen Network (www.SmallScreenNetwork.com). His videos provide easily accessed information and instructions on how anybody can make great cocktails.